fragile

30 Days of HOPE
for the Anxious Heart

Samantha Arroyo

Carpenter's Son Publishing

Published by Carpenter's Son Publishing, Franklin, Tennessee.

Published in association with Larry Carpenter of Christian Book Services, LLC. www.christianbookservices.com.

All Scripture quotations, unless otherwise indicated, are taken from the Holy Bible, New International Version®, NIV®. Copyright © 1973, 1978, 1984 by Biblica, Inc.™ Used by permission of Zondervan. All rights reserved worldwide. www. zondervan.com. The "NIV" and "New International Version" are trademarks registered in the United States Patent and Trademark Office by Biblica, Inc.™

Scripture quotations marked (ESV) are from the ESV® Bible (The Holy Bible, English Standard Version®), copyright © 2001 by Crossway, a publishing ministry of Good News Publishers. Used by permission. All rights reserved.

Taken from *NIV Study Bible – Supplementary Materials* by Zondervan. Copyright © 2002 by Zondervan. Used by permission of Zondervan. www.zondervan.com. All rights reserved.

Taken from *The Strongest NIV Exhaustive Concordance* by Edward W. Goodrick and John R. Kohlenberger III. Copyright © 1999, 1990 by Zondervan. Used by permission of Zondervan. www.zondervan.com. All rights reserved.

Taken from *Facing Your Giants* by Max Lucado. Copyright © 2006 by Max Lucado. Used by permission of Thomas Nelson. www.thomasnelson.com. All rights reserved.

Cover Design by Suzanne Lawing

Interior Design by Mark Neubauer

Edited by Tammy Kling

Printed in the United States of America

978-1-942587-03-3

Author photo by Kyle M. Reilly of University Smile

Cover photo by Stephanie Ma

"All I can say is WOW! I will even use it as an ongoing reference in my library for message prep & counseling tools. This is incredible! OUTSTANDING!"

—Pastor Todd Spain, Crossroads Church

DEDICATED TO

My Heavenly Father.
For never giving up on this weary, stubborn, oh-so fragile soul.
I love you more than life.

Special Thanks to

My husband.
Your intense patience and unshakable faith have seen me through some of my deepest valleys and darkest moments. I'm so thankful that God trusted me with your heart. Thank you for your support, encouragement, and for the countless hours you spent helping me edit these pages. You are my hero. I love you more.

My mom.
Your resilient, steadfast prayers throughout my entire life have everything to do with where I am today. I'd be a mess without your wisdom and friendship. Thank you for believing in me.

My dad.
You've always made home a safe place to run to when the world seemed too scary. Thank you for the sacrifices you've made, for always putting our family first, and for reminding me to keep my eyes on the prize.

My brother.
You've always seen *me*. Thank you for pushing me toward confidence. I love you to the moon and back.

Tammy Sollenberger.
You allowed God to speak through you. Thank you for saying the things I needed to hear and not necessarily what I wanted to hear, and for contributing to the challenges put forth in this book. You have been instrumental in my healing. Thanks for turning the lights on.

CONTENTS

SAMANTHA ARROYO

LETTER

Dear Fragile Soul,

So here you are. A little battered. A little bruised. *A lot* weary. Your heart aches for hope; your spirit hungers for rest. Relief from the strangling thoughts, the agonizing fear, the relentless worry that holds your mind hostage. You've become a prisoner in your own skin and feel you have no choice but to make your damp, musty, lonely cell inhabitable—comfortable, at best. You might as well hang up some pictures and throw down a rug. After all, there's no escape. It's a life sentence.

Right?

If you're like me, you aren't experiencing everyday anxieties. Rather, you're imprisoned by *chronic* worry.

Chronic worry ravaged my soul and poisoned my thoughts, crippling me into submission day after day. It kept me from eating. It kept me in bed. It made me sick. And, at its worst, kept me from working. I felt damaged, fractured, shattered into a million splintered pieces that couldn't possibly be put back together. But God began to show me in small doses that I wasn't crushed—I was only cracked. I was fragile—a delicate, sensitive soul that needed to be handled with care. *His care.*

Then God led me on a journey through His Word, revealing the truth about worry and anxiety.

And about the freedom made available through His Son. And what that freedom looks like.

The pages you are holding led to my personal healing, to whole-ness. My anxiety may not be perfectly piloted, but I've found solid ground and steady footing for the first time in more than a decade. As I wrote each chapter, I prayed for you—the person who might one day find refuge in the words God gave me. I prayed for the words as they bled onto the pages and for the emotions, raw and real, that spilled from this fragile soul to yours. I prayed the Lord would move my fingers across the keys—each stroke under the power and control of His mighty hand. I prayed I would be so far removed from this work, this labor of healing, so only His redeeming grace is felt.

I wrote through a blur of tears and often had to stop, submitting once again to my anxious thoughts. Afraid, at times, what God might reveal to me: the truths about myself that I'd have to face head-on. But He brought me through it—to the Promised Land on the other side of the desert plain I had been wandering. He showed me grace.

I pray you see Jesus here—between the lines, in the margins. I pray you see His fingerprints on the binding and that you sense His presence and deep affection for you. That you feel the soft caress of His grace and the sweetness of His patience.

As we begin this journey into the truth of God's Word, please know that these pages should only be read as *part* of a more robust treatment plan. Chronic anxiety is a mental illness. It's compli-cated and can manifest itself in a number of ways. As much as you and I would like to wrestle our emotions into obedience, there are biological and chemical causes at play that are outside of our immediate control. What you are suffering with isn't necessarily a choice. It isn't merely a character defect or faith obstacle. And it isn't just a biological malfunction either. Those are easy answers. It's not black and white, so it should be treated with as much care and respect as a physical illness.

Think of clinical anxiety as you would diabetes. Although rare, some diabetics make significant changes to their current lifestyles, which involve weight management as well as exercise and diet modification, and consequently enter remission—ridding themselves of the need for medication.[1] Others may make the same changes yet still require ongoing medical treatment. Is the diabetic to blame when he or she must continue to rely on insulin? Certainly not.

In the same way, those with chronic anxiety undergo different treatment plans. I encourage you—no, I implore you—to consult with your health care provider and a therapist if you are struggling with crippling emotions. There is no shame in consulting a physician. It doesn't make you weak, and it doesn't make your faith weak either.

This book will help guide you through the spiritual elements of worry and anxiety, but be sure not to neglect the physical and emotional components. All three are critical if you want to experience healing. Read this guide one chapter at a time. *Healing is a delicate process, and it cannot be rushed.*

You must also know that anxiety is not sinful. Worry, however, *is.* By studying the Greek and Hebrew translations of these words throughout the Old and New Testaments, God opened my eyes to a striking difference: anxiety is a noun, an emotion; worry is a verb, a behavior.[2] Emotions are not sinful. It's what you *do* with those emotions and feelings that can result in sin.

I say all this to set the foundation for the hard work ahead. In my personal opinion, the spiritual element of healing is most important. I did a lot of heavy lifting years ago when my anxiety manifested itself into a life-threatening eating disorder. I tried to control it, grapple with, subdue it. I *managed* it. Managing takes a lot of effort and is entirely dependent on what *you* do and do not do—it doesn't give God any room to work. So it was only a matter of time until it exposed itself somewhere else. It wasn't until I released my vice grip, repented for not relinquishing control years prior, and sought God's wisdom and healing that the anxiety began to unravel.

God could rid you of your anxiety in an instant. He could relieve you from ever having an anxious thought again. Because He is God and all things are made possible through Him (see Mark 10:27). Or, like me, like most, He could use your crisis as a faith catalyst. He could use this dark place to reveal Himself to you in a bright and brilliant way—a way you've never known. Perhaps you will become so intimately entangled with the Father's love as a result of this adversity because, until now, you've never had to lean hard into His grace.

Fragile Soul, you are not broken beyond repair. You are merely a cracked pot in the hands of the Master Potter. He will form you and shape you and smooth out the ravine in your heart that's been carved by worry. One day, I pray you look up from these pages and see that God's hand on your life never lifted. That He was with you every step—and back step—along this messy road.

I pray you sense His closeness here. I pray you'll open your heart to what the Lord has to say. Allow Him to reach into the scariest parts. The disheveled parts. The ugliest parts. He is the key to releasing the chains of worry. There's no reason for them to have a hold on your life forever. God promises freedom in His Son, Jesus Christ. Your journey to healing, freedom, and security can start today if you allow God to enter your heart and transform your soul. Allow Him to have His way.

Are you ready? Are you ready to begin healing?

Then, come. Let's begin. I know it isn't easy. It may even be the scariest thing you've ever done. But know that I am praying for you every step of the way.

From one fragile yet empowered soul to another,
Samantha

FRAGILE

faith

FRAGILE

1

FALL

Strengthen the feeble hands, steady the knees that give way; say to those with fearful hearts, "Be strong, do not fear; your God will come, he will come with vengeance; with divine retribution he will come to save you."
—Isaiah 35:3–4

Heart, mind, and body like snow-laden branches sagging—hanging—just above the ground on the cusp of snapping. Soft breezes, gentle movements cause you to creak and sway dangerously. Breath comes slowly, shallow. It's crippling. The hands that once held steady, tremble. The knees that once held firm rest huddled against your chest; your feeble arms wrapped tight around. When the limbs are weak, the body is weak. Coupled with a fluttering heart, the weight of weakness is nearly unbearable.

I was there. You *are* there. You feel like a dinghy floating helplessly on an ocean of fear, and land is but a mirage. You pray for rescue, and yet, it's as if your prayers are bouncing off the floors of heaven.

I couldn't eat. I could hardly work. I cried as my husband left the house and cried as I drove to the cubicle I worked so hard to gain. I had nightmares. Each day felt like a chore—a feat to overcome.

But like a functioning addict, I masked my trembling hands with energized hand gestures and fast-paced typing. Coworkers, oblivious to my thoughts that came forth like an oncoming train, said I looked tired, pale.

"It's just a headache," I'd occasionally reply.

It wasn't a lie—my head ached with the noise. The loud whirring of anxiety. Like a song stuck on repeat.

Like the tight creaking of snow-covered branches, I began cracking. In front of my husband in the morning when it hurt to get out of bed. In front of my parents on a Christmas weekend getaway. Until one day, I snapped. It wasn't a clean break—it was messy. Shards of a broken, weak, and tired heart pooled beneath my eyelids and tumbled down cheeks that hadn't felt the pull of a smile in months. It was just past six o'clock in the evening, and I was already slipping into pajamas, intending to crawl beneath the sheets within the hour. My husband climbed the stairs, and we met on the landing. One look was all it took for him to know I was crumbling. Right there—in front of his eyes. I collapsed into his arms and mumbled the words—the strongest words—I've ever spoken: "I need help."

My cry wasn't to please anyone else or another attempt to cover up the symptoms. It was for me—for the first time in nearly a decade, *I* wanted healing. True, pure, redemptive, God-breathed healing. To finally taste true freedom from the bitter sting of a broken past.

That evening began my journey. A journey I'm still walking. I felt weak in that moment and the moments that followed: The moment I called a therapist. The moment I decided to face my messy past. The moment I decided I was too tired to fight alone.

My life didn't start falling apart when I fell into my husband's arms.

It started to fall into place.

"Your God will come," Isaiah says. "He will come with vengeance; with divine retribution he will come to *save* you" (Isa. 35:4, emphasis mine). The word "save" in Hebrew, can also mean to deliver, rescue.[1] He won't just help you *manage* the worry. He'll *pull* you out from underneath its ruthless control.

He'll free you. Free you from slaving under the heavy hand of anxiety, worry, and hopelessness. But you have to fall into His arms before you can begin to put the pieces back together. You must thrust your trembling hands towards the heavens, like a child reaching for her daddy.

It's time to let Him pick you up.

> **He won't just help you *manage* the worry. He'll *pull* you out from underneath its ruthless control.**

You may feel as though you've lost all control. That you've hit rock bottom. But perhaps God has allowed you to land in this place—whatever this place looks like—so that you have no other choice but to cling to Him. So that you have to look *up*.

Trust Him. Lean into His arms. Surrender. Surrender today. Right now. Wherever this moment has you; it's the very first step toward freedom.

Father, I come before You today with a heavy heart. I have weak hands and trembling knees, and life seems insurmountable. But You came to save and to give freedom to fragile hearts like mine. Help me, Father, to believe that promise. Help me to surrender my worry, not just now, but tomorrow and the day after that and

the day after that. Help me to collapse into Your arms and trust that there is no safer place to fall. Help me to surrender. Amen.

CHALLENGE

Congratulations, you just surrendered. Tomorrow, you must surrender again. And you'll need to be reminded because what you read today will likely be a distant memory in just a few hours, clouded out by anxious thoughts. Make it easy for yourself. Find a scrap piece of paper or a colorful sticky note and write *surrender* on it. Place it on your alarm clock, so you'll see it as dawn breaks. Before your feet hit the floor in the morning make a commitment to *surrender.*

2

WORRY

During the fourth watch of the night Jesus went out to them, walking on the lake. When the disciples saw him walking on the lake, they were terrified. "It's a ghost," they said, and cried out in fear.
But Jesus immediately said to them: "Take courage! It is I. Don't be afraid."
"Lord, if it's you," Peter replied, "tell me to come to you on the water."
"Come," he said.
Then Peter got down out of the boat, walked on the water and came toward Jesus. But when he saw the wind, he was afraid and, beginning to sink, cried out, "Lord, save me!"
Immediately Jesus reached out his hand and caught him. "You of little faith," he said, "why did you doubt?"
And when they climbed into the boat, the wind died down.
—Matthew 14:25–32

Wind: it gently rustles the leaves on a sunny day. It leaves catastrophe in its wake, tearing off roofs and tossing vehicles into the air like plastic toy cars. You can't see it coming or predict where it's going. It swells, like waves, washing through, over, and around everything it passes. No surface, not an inch of skin, left untouched.

Wind.

It can caress without leaving a trace of evidence, send chills through your bones, seep cold beneath a wool jacket, or blow hard and fast like the roar of jetliner, violently uprooting the sturdiest oak.

Wind: a palpable portrait of anxiety.

Like a cool breeze, anxiety can creep in small—beginning as a soft, innocent thought. Or it can send you immediately to your knees, struggling for shallow breath. It can roar so loudly, so powerfully, that people appear to be props in an elaborate, silent movie. They talk, move, push papers across your desk, and yet you can hardly hear them. You are only aware of the deafening sound of uninvited thoughts that relentlessly attack, distract, and exhaust.

Peter stepped out onto the water. He trusted. He believed. He was the only one in the boat to step out and move forward in faith. He longed to be near His Savior. And yet, as he put one foot in front of the other, he caught a glimpse of the wind pulling the waves higher as it rushed across the surface of the water and tangled itself in the sails. He *saw*. And he *panicked*.

The witness to this unforeseen event writes that Peter *saw* the wind. But he also writes that Peter and the others *saw* Jesus. In these verses, the word "saw" is derived from two different Greek words. When the disciples *saw* Jesus on the water, the Greek word used is *horaō*, which can mean to see, notice, or perceive.[1]

Later, when Peter *saw* the wind, the Greek word used is *blepō*, which means "to see, look at; to watch out, beware, pay attention."[2]

Similar, yes, but vastly different. To illustrate the difference, consider the two English words, "listen" and "hear." When you *hear* something, your brain registers a sound. You may have heard someone speaking, but are unsure who spoke. You may have heard a crash, but you are unsure where it came from. When you *listen*, however, you concentrate. You are attentive and intensely focused. You're *fixated*.

Peter saw (horaō) Jesus, but he *saw* (blepō) the wind. He took his eyes off Jesus and was, instead, fixated on the wind as it raced across the water.

**His anxiety was instant.
But he sank *slowly*.**

It appears to have been only for a moment. But, as you know, a moment is all it takes for anxiety to take hold, squeezing the air from your lungs.

Before Peter courageously climbed out of the boat, he rested his eyes on Jesus. And as Peter's foot grazed the stormy seas, he found sure footing.

But the wind churned and the seas roared all around him, so Peter took his eyes off Jesus and turned his face into the wind. His eyes grew wide, fixating on the angry, boiling spans of the deep. And he *began* to sink. His anxiety was instant. But he sank *slowly*.

Perhaps the water rushed over his feet, past his ankles and up his shins, his mind focused purely on the wind—the storm—that tossed the waters violently from side to side and whipped at his clothing. At that moment, nothing could break his attention. Fear paralyzed him. He stood there, the waters still rising, until he suddenly became aware of his fate. He looked down, the water now past his knees, and cried out. "Lord, save me!"

Immediately, Jesus extended His hand and caught him. *Immediately*.

Did Jesus pull him up, firmly planting Peter's feet back on the water? Did they walk back to the boat together? Did Peter collapse into his Savior's arms? We don't know. But we *do* know that Jesus caught him.

And that Peter called out to Jesus *before* rescue came.

Don't you see? As disciples, Jesus calls us out of the boat. He calls us toward Him. And it's only a matter of time before He calls you to cross a stormy sea.

Will you look *at* Him or will you look *to* Him?

Right now, you face waves of anxiety. They crash around me, too. And even the waves of anxiety come in different shapes and sizes. Maybe they are waves of divorce, death, or a broken relationship. Maybe your storm resembles a violent squall, hitting hard and fast and unexpectedly. Or maybe your storm is more like a constant, howling wind that never lets up. Never tires. As the waves splash around your ankles, you find yourself lending your attention and your thoughts to them—and they begin to drown you in worry.

When the winds come—and they will come, whether gentle or catastrophic—will you catch a *glimpse* of Jesus, or will you *focus intently* on the cross, on His grace, on His power? Will you look *at* Him or will you look *to* Him? However great the storm, however dark the sky, I pray you utter these three little words: "Lord, save me."

Today we surrender as we did yesterday. Together. And tomorrow, we'll do the same. Because surrender requires daily decision. It's ongoing and essential to your fight—and, in time, freedom from worry's hold on your life. Reach out your hand. Call on the name of Jesus for rescue. And one day, you will be free.

Lord, I come to you once again in complete surrender. Lord, save

me. Save me from the overwhelming thoughts and crippling anxiety that ultimately cause me to worry time and time again. I trust that You will catch me if I allow You to take control. You are strong, and You are able. I am not past rescuing. Help me believe that. Lord, You know my heart. You know how hard this is for me. Thank You for Your patience. Help me fight; fight for me, Lord. Help me keep my eyes fixed on You, Your glory, Your power, and Your overwhelming majesty. Amen.

CHALLENGE

Purchase a journal. One that's pleasant to look at. Consider buying more than one: one for work, one for home. Use it for the next twenty-nine days (and beyond) to keep a record of your anxious thoughts. Describe your exhaustion and fear. What does it feel like? What does it look like? When does anxiety strike? What triggers it? After all, the battle cannot be won without knowing whom or what you're up against. You must be familiar with the enemy's tricks and strategies. How else can you devise a plan of attack? But most importantly, study Bible verses about worry and anxiety, and scribble them into your journal along with your descriptions of anxiety. You'll discover verses you've never read and rediscover the familiar from a different perspective.

3

HE WEPT

*When Mary reached the place where Jesus was and saw him, she
fell at his feet and said, "Lord, if you had been here, my brother
would not have died."
When Jesus saw her weeping, and the Jews who had come
along with her also weeping, he was deeply moved in spirit and
troubled. "Where have you laid him?" he asked.
"Come and see, Lord," they replied.
Jesus wept.
—John 11:32–35*

Curled up in the stairwell, just past the first landing, hidden from
those who passed by. Just far enough away to flee at the sound of
feet climbing stairs. That's where I found a bit of refuge, solace. The
third stair up from the landing. I would sit with my chin against
my knees and rock back and forth. And I would pray, pray, pray.
Deliver me, Lord.

Clutching the steering wheel with windows rolled up and the
sound of worship filling every crevice, every empty space, I would
wail aloud, the tears blurring the road that led to the office. And
I would beg, beg, beg. *Take this from me, Lord.*

The sound of a familiar "good morning" over the telephone. What did "good" feel like? I had forgotten. My voice cracked, giving way to tears unstoppable. A stomach filled only with coffee, a body running on caffeine fumes. I hadn't eaten in days. Not because I didn't want to—because I couldn't. The smells were repulsive. The nausea relentless. And for the twenty-five-minute commute, I would cry, cry, cry. *I need You, Father.*

Mary and Martha also presented their needs to Jesus: "Lord, the one you love is sick" (see John 11:3). They did not ask that He come. They trusted Him, knowing He would do what He felt best. Perhaps, like me, they assumed His reaction would mirror their own. Surely Jesus would weep over their distress when He learned His dear friend was fatally ill—and would come.

Jesus loved Lazarus. They had a close relationship. He loved Mary and Martha, too, and it was *because* of that love, He stayed where He was two more days.[1] He didn't rush to where they were. He stayed put. Their need was great, their desperation heavy, making Jesus' response seem scandalous at the very least. Yet Jesus was not concerned with how His response was perceived. He waited. He stayed in Bethany. Because He was, and still is, more concerned with the Father's will than our immediate and long-term comfort.

When Jesus finally arrived in Bethany, He was met by Martha. Mary stayed in the house. "Lord, if you had been here . . ." she says. *If only.* "But I know that even now God will give you whatever you ask" (John 11:21–22).

The exchange that follows is packed with such theological significance, but I want to draw your attention to a small nugget in the verses that follow . . .

After Martha shares a few words with Jesus, she returns to the house to gather her sister Mary. Jesus stayed where He was and waited for Mary to come. When Mary heard that Jesus was waiting for her, she rose quickly and ran to Him. Those who were in the home with her followed, assuming she was going to her brother's tomb to mourn. But instead, she collapsed at Jesus' feet (see John 11:28–32).

Dust plumed around her as her hands slapped the cracked, dry earth. She knelt before the same feet—now soiled from days of travel—that she had bathed with oils and perfumes, and wiped dry with her hair (see John 11:2).

"Lord, if you had been here, my brother would not have died" (v. 32). If only. *If only.* Do you hear the heaviness in her heart? It was too late. Her brother was gone.

Had He not received her message? Had He not cared? Had He not understood how dire the need?

In that day, many Jews believed that the soul remained with the body for three days before departing.[2] It had been four days. Perhaps Mary had held out hope even after Lazarus passed. But four days? Four days was just too long. Her hope was crushed.

Jesus could not have appeared more catastrophically late.

One brief sentence was all Mary could muster before the tears took over. She moaned with brokenness. There was nothing left to give; her heart had shattered into a thousand pieces and nothing—no one—seemed to have the means to repair it.

Those alongside her began to weep as well. A loud expression of grief, of wailing. This was Jewish tradition: to weep loudly with those who mourned.[3] And as Jesus took in the scene, He was deeply moved.

And He wept. The original language tells us that He didn't weep as the others did. Rather, He "shed tears." [4] They came softer, quieter, perhaps even silently. He felt their pain. He empathized. Lazarus was not a mere stranger; he was a very dear friend.

Just as *you* are.

Jesus could have healed Lazarus from afar as he had the Centurion's servant (Luke 7:1–10). But He chose not to. He could have left for Lazarus' home right away when he received the news. But He chose to stay where He was two more days. He could have reassured Mary and Martha right away with the same words He spoke in Bethany after hearing the news, "This sickness will not end in death. No, it is for God's glory so that God's Son may be glorified through it" (John 11:4). Words that Mary and Martha had not heard but desperately hoped to hear.

But He didn't . . .

Though He knew the grave would not hold Lazarus much longer, He still wept with those who mourned (see Rom. 12:15). His heart breaks for you, too. Over your pain, your anxiety, your hopelessness, and desperation—all of it. This story contains tremendous theology. The weight of these verses takes great study. But that tiny verse gets my attention every time: Jesus wept. Not an uncontrollable, deep, hopeless cry, but a quiet weeping. Oh, how His heart hurt for those He loved.

It still does because His heart hurts for your pain.

Jesus was not there to grieve; He was there to free and to heal. In the same way, He has come to deliver you—us—from the pain, distress, and uncertainty that clouds the everyday. He wants to push back the blinds so that we can see life's beauty and meaning once again. He sees the tears that soak your pillow each night. He hears your desperate cries that shatter the night's silence. He sees your fists hit the ground, as Mary's did. He hears your cries, whispered in secret.

Oh, if they only knew what I was about to do. If they could see the rest of the picture, they'd understand. I am working. I am moving. I am going to glorify My Father through them.

With a crowd of witnesses before Him, Jesus called Lazarus from the tomb. Wilting, wrinkled linens clung to Lazarus' body as he emerged. Witnesses, who wouldn't have been there if Jesus healed Lazarus *before* he died, saw him come forth from the tomb.

And do you know what happened next?

"Many of the Jews who had come to visit Mary, and had seen what Jesus did, put their faith in him" (John 11:45).

They believed. The Lord freed not only Mary and Martha from their temporary sadness and Lazarus from his illness and consequent death—He restored many because He was able to use their pain for His Father's glory.

If one person came to know Jesus, was restored, renewed, and would one day live eternally with our Father, would it not all be worth it?

Jesus knows your pain and may very well be weeping alongside you. Chronic anxiety is not part of His plan for your life. Just as death was never meant to be part of the garden. But if you allow Him, if you surrender your pain, He will use it. Whether today, tomorrow, or a decade from now, He will use it.

Jesus *allowed* those He loved to suffer emotionally. He *allowed* them to weep so that His Father could receive glory before the largest number of witnesses. So, ultimately, more would be adopted into His kingdom.

> **He'll use your sorrow for an eternal purpose.**

Surrender today as you have been. Give Him your sorrow. Collapse at His feet. Wail. Cry. He's heard it. He's seen it. He's *felt* it. Trust that He's moving. And thank Him for what He'll do through you and for how He'll use your sorrow for an eternal purpose.

Father, I don't know what You're doing. I don't understand why this pain won't let up. I don't know why my heart is anxious. I feel as though I have no control, and to be honest, I feel like I'm already too far gone. Like I'm four days dead. Like You're too late. Even so, please use my sorrow, my emptiness, my pain to glorify Yourself. My prayer is the same: save me, deliver me. But may it be in Your time and according to Your perfect will. As Jesus said before summoning Lazarus from the tomb, "Father, I thank you that you have heard me" (v. 41). Amen.

CHALLENGE

Thank Jesus for how He is moving. Even though you can't see it. Even though you can't feel it. Thank Him for hearing your cries, your screams, your silent prayers. It's hard—you may be angry because you have not felt an ounce of relief, but continue to pray with thanksgiving. It's a balm for worry (see Phil. 4:6). Thank Him in advance for His healing and for what He'll do through you.

4

YOU

And being in anguish, he prayed more earnestly, and his sweat
was like drops of blood falling to the ground.
—Luke 22:44

Brain sweating.

It can happen while guiding your cart through the produce department. In the locked corporate bathroom, unsteady hands gripping the lip of the porcelain pedestal sink. In your windowless cubical. In the lonely quiet. In public. At the playground. At the midnight hour beneath layers of blanket.

You can't think fast enough. Or rather, you can't keep up with the grueling onslaught of words, images, and fears that consume and overwhelm. They're unforgiving. Relentless.

It's as if your brain sweats with exertion.

Uninvited tears seep from beneath tired lids. Sometimes they come quietly. Other times they come with an exasperated heavy sigh from deep within. You've prayed He would come and relinquish you from this misery. *Take it from me*, you pray. If only Jesus would make a grand entrance, unlock the iron handcuffs, and set you free. But no. Today you're left shackled within your own skin, imprisoned by your thoughts, and escape seems impossible.

You have a drug of choice, don't you? I did.

In those moments you begin to worry about worrying. You worry about not being able to fall asleep. You panic that a passerby might witness the beads of sweat forming on your brow. You worry the cashier will notice your trembling hands as you extend them to pay for your items. You count the minutes until the end of the work day. You attempt to distract your mind with mindless games like crossword puzzles, Sudoku, and word searches. Or perhaps you reach for another drink, surf the Internet, turn on the television, or go shopping. You have a drug of choice, don't you? I did.

Luke records Jesus' prayer on the lower slopes of the Mount of Olives.[1] As Jesus knelt with His face to the ground, He prayed, "Father, if you are willing, take this cup from me; yet not my will, but yours be done" (Luke 22:42). He foresaw the cup of suffering—the brutality of the cross, most assume. However, physical torment He could withstand. The cup He feared was His Father's wrath and the pain He would endure shouldering the sins of the world: past, present, and future. Your sins. My sins. Your worry. My worry.

In the verses that follow, Jesus is overcome with "anguish." This Greek word is used only once in the New Testament: *agōnia*. It means anguish, anxiety, a severe mental struggle. Agony. A struggle for victory.[2] A physical wrestling far, far greater than anything we've ever experienced while navigating through grocery-store aisles. But our Lord did not distract His weighted emotions, as we often do. He did not turn to a preferred coping mechanism.

Instead, He "prayed more earnestly." *Earnestly*, while it means just that,[3] is derived from a Greek word that means "stretched out."[4] Jesus stretched His prayers. Like a rope without slack, like an hand outstretched, He prayed more strenuously. With eagerness and fervor and intensity of mind. He didn't let up. He didn't give in to the anxiety. He wrestled with it, yes. The mental struggle came, yes. But He did not willingly let the thoughts seep in without notice and morph into active worry. He took them captive and was, therefore, not overcome by them.

Hebrews 5:7 says, "During the days of Jesus' life on earth, he offered up prayers and petitions with loud cries and tears to the one who could save him from death, and he was heard because of his reverent submission." This, a direct echo to Christ's agony in the garden.[5] He did not waver in His determination or shrink away from God's will even though His soul was overwhelmed with sorrow and distress (see Matt. 26:38).

Luke, a doctor by profession,[6] described Jesus' anguish as so severe that His sweat was like drops of blood. Of all the Gospel accounts, Luke is the only author to mention this detail. Yet, he's a physician. And so, perhaps such details are more apparent to him. Some believe Jesus sweat large droplets of perspiration, similar in appearance to blood. But maybe His sweat mingled with blood as a result of severe anguish and mental strain. It's actually a diagnosable physical ailment called hematidrosis.[7] It would not be unlikely that our Savior, a sinless man who was about to inherit the world's mockery, sin, shame, and evil, would fall ill to this.

We don't know *how* His prayers became more earnest. We don't know what He said. But we know He gathered enough strength to rise to His feet and go back to His disciples who had fallen asleep, exhausted from sorrow (see Luke 22:45).

"Why are you sleeping?" He asked them. "Get up and pray so that you will not fall into temptation" (Luke 22:46). Can we not presume that this is precisely what Jesus Christ *just did*? Certainly He felt the temptation to give His anxious mind to worry—consciously choosing to focus on fear and the spiritual agony to come. But instead, He prayed Himself *out* of temptation.

He didn't give up. He didn't give in. *Even when the anxiousness returned.*

Matthew and Mark testify that Jesus went back a second time and prayed with the same passion and sincerity. And then a third time (see Matt. 26:36–46 and Mark 14:32–42).

He didn't give up. He didn't give in. *Even when the anxiousness returned.*

Jesus felt anxious, yes. But anxiousness is a feeling, an involuntary response mechanism. It protects us. It's what propels us to swerve out of the way of an oncoming vehicle or keep a safe distance from the edge of a cliff.

Jesus was about to face certain, excruciating death, and His Father would forsake Him. His flesh was anxious. But He didn't worry. Worry is a behavior. Worry is the sin—not anxiousness. Worry is misplaced trust. It's being concerned about what may or may not happen in the future.

His telling us not to worry (Luke 12:22–34) prior to this event is more than a command; it's a loving invitation. An invitation to live a life brimming with possibility, not ominous threat. An invitation to draw closer to the Father through prayer when we begin to feel anxious.

But Philippians 4:6, you may be thinking. *It says we are not to be anxious.*

I wrestled with that verse for years. "Do not be anxious," it reads. It seemed too lofty a request. Too unrealistic. Too supernatural. But then I discovered a freeing truth when I studied what the word "anxious" meant in the Greek language. In this particular case, "anxious" is translated from the same word used for worry: *merimnaō.*[8] Jesus wasn't telling us not to *feel* anxious. Jesus was telling us not to *live* worried.

This is a critical distinction, and it transformed my faith in Christ, giving me a fresh perspective and greater understanding for what Jesus was so desperately trying to communicate.

Jesus wasn't telling us not to *feel* anxious. Jesus was telling us not to *live* worried.

Jesus faced certain death. And yet, the words *what if* did not cloud the future. Worry did not seize His heart. Rather, He relinquished His anxiousness to the Father. And He got back on His own two feet. Three times He knelt and three times He got back up. He wrestled with anxiety, but in the end, though doused in sweat, He was victorious over the temptation—the temptation to worry and ultimately deviate from His Father's plan.

The next time you think that Jesus doesn't understand, may you remember this passage. Remember the garden. Remember His wrestling—*alone*, in the dark, as His closest friends *slept* unaware of His suffering. And respond as He did. Pray. Pray *hard*. Pray *earnestly*. Pray until you can stand back up. It may take five minutes or five hours. Regardless, we must heed the call in 1 Thessalonians 5:17 to pray without ceasing.

Where your eyes are fixed, so your
faith will follow.

**Pray until you can stand
back up.**

So fix your eyes on Jesus. Don't turn
your face toward anxiety, toward the
waves; turn instead to the Father. In war, to defeat the enemy you
must outsmart or overwhelm them. You have to know their plans,
their tactics, their routes. You have to know *who* they are. So, name
it. Name your worry. Name your fear. Name your enemy.

And then pray earnestly against it.

**Jesus, it is not Your will that I live worried. This anxiety plagues
me. For the average person, it comes and goes like a tide, but it
lingers with me. Overruns me like a tsunami. I take great comfort in knowing that You've experienced anxiety to a far greater
extent than I have. And You defeated it. I pray that my prayers
become more earnest—like Yours. I pray that they become more
powerful in faith, overflowing with conviction. Thank You for
being who You are. Thank You for journeying to the cross. For
willingly climbing up that tree to pay for my sin, my worry. Help
me keep Satan from gaining a foothold in my mind today. Amen.**

CHALLENGE

When we come face to face with our insecurities, when anxiety
rises like a giant before us, it is easy to say, "I can't help feeling this
way." It takes courage to fight. Even when you feel as though you
are in a losing battle, fight. You may lose the battle, but there *will* be
battles you win, which will ultimately help you win the war. Fight
with prayer, as Jesus did. Jesus knows *exactly* how you feel—and
has felt anxiety to a far greater extent, to the point of shedding
blood. Follow His tactics. Before you rise in the morning, look at

that sticky note on your alarm clock. Surrender. But linger a little longer now. With the covers pulled up beneath your chin, earnestly surrender. Like a rope without slack, giving it all you have, as Jesus did. And when you turn in for the night, pray against the anxious thoughts that threaten to keep you awake. Pray earnestly until sweet sleep overwhelms you.

That's a battle well fought.

5

SUFFERING

How long, O Lord? Will you forget me forever? How long will you hide your face from me? How long must I wrestle with my thoughts and every day have sorrow in my heart? How long will my enemy triumph over me?
—Psalm 13:1–2

Twinkling lights cast a soft glow against the freshly fallen snow as the familiar sound of holiday carols danced toward the night sky. But I scarcely noticed. The crackling fire did little more than keep my mittened fingers toasty warm. I wasn't interested in huddled conversation, but I forced my body language to imply otherwise. The town's annual Christmas tree lit up the center of Main Street, and horse-drawn carriages moved whimsically through the beachside town. A cozy summer retreat, alive again with the magic of the holiday. Yet I could relish none of it.

Like David, I wrestled with my thoughts. Every day seemed to wash me in sorrow. *How long?* I begged, as David did.

Brute force kept me physically present that day. But as evening clawed at my façade, my strength to hold it all together sapped.

I was sitting cross-legged on the hotel bed when my shoulders began to tremble. The mask was crumbling. This time, before two sets of eyes: my husband's and my mother's.

The tremors came harder, faster. They were uncontrollable. My mom pulled me back against her chest and rocked me. Back and forth, back and forth. Like a child. Tears came slowly at first, and as she turned to face me, more heavily.

My husband looked up from his reading and, seeing my tears, hurried to my side. I struggled for breath and sorrow spilled from my tired eyes.

I had made a mistake at the office, and I couldn't let it go. I agonized over it. It was something I couldn't change, yet the misplaced pen stroke—the grammatical mishap—wouldn't release its tormenting grip on my mind. I held it; it held me.

That faux pas stole a three-day weekend with my family. One filled with Christmas festivities, shimmering lights, traditional carols, boisterous laughter, trolley rides, and heartfelt conversation.

It was taken from me. Stolen. That's what worry does—it keeps you from actively participating, from functioning.

My thoughts—the enemy's choice weapon—triumphed over me because I had little fight left in my bones. My howling that night, like David's, was sapped of patience and strength. There was such anguish in my heart. The stressor, the *irrational* fear, was weeks old. But I was *still* gripped by it. Obsessed. Terrified of making another mistake.

How long?

We ask this of the Father often, don't we? *How much longer must I wait? How much longer must I endure? How much longer must I fight?* God has seen us through glorious moments of victory, but in times of long-suffering, those victories are nothing more than blurry, distant memories.

You pray for deliverance, but when your prayers aren't met with immediate rescue, you begin to feel the way the enemy *wants* you to feel: forgotten. And worse, forgotten by *God.*

I love how the Bible doesn't just paint a pretty picture of David's triumphs; it also provides a window into his moments of tremendous weakness. Throughout the Psalms, David calls on God for deliverance and mercy. We read how he drenches his couch

> **Christianity isn't a bulletproof vest. We are targeted. We have a very real enemy who seeks to destroy us.**

with tears (Ps. 6:6), and we empathize. There's such comfort in this: that the very same man who took down a giant and ruled as king—a man after God's own heart—also succumbed, at times, to worry.

As children of God, we are not immune to trouble. Christianity isn't a bulletproof vest. We are targeted. We have a very real enemy who seeks to destroy us. Those who don't know Christ as Savior are right where Satan wants them. Therefore, it is in Satan's best interest to set a keen eye on those who claim Jesus Christ as Lord and King.

Satan doesn't waste his time. He knows he can't have your soul, so he'll do everything he can to make you as ineffective for Christ as possible. And if he's successful in his mission, you won't win any more souls for Christ. You have a target on your back, friend. So did David. So did Job. And like Job, Satan has set out to ruin you for no other reason than to get you to blame God (Job 2:3–4).[1]

He's smart. He's subtle. He's cunning. And he's ever so patient. He'll wait for just the right moment—when you're most vulnerable. That's when he'll strike, preventing you from living the life Jesus sacrificed his own for.

Satan has set out to ruin you for no other reason than to get you to blame God.

David *knew* rescue. He had tasted deliverance. He had felt grace and seen redemption. And though he cried out from a broken heart, he concluded his prayer in Psalm 13 with confidence.

"But," he says. "*But* I trust in your unfailing love; my heart rejoices in your salvation. I will sing to the LORD for **he has been good to me**" (Ps. 13:5–6, emphasis mine).

Yes, our God has been good to us. Indeed, He has.

And He will draw near to you now.

You may feel like your life is unraveling. And your prayers may wear thin, too. But choose to speak truth into your life, as David did. Choose to *remember*. Don't let the enemy steal your memories of God's provision like he has stolen days meant for joy.

Even if you succumbed to worry today, end your day with a "BUT."

BUT *GOD.*

The enemy may have robbed you of today . . . BUT GOD.

My heart is filled with sorrow, BUT God will restore me.

My mind is wrought with worry, BUT God will deliver me.
My body is weak with fatigue, BUT God will renew me.

Because God has been good to me.

Trust that. Lean into His promises. He hasn't failed you yet, and He isn't about to fail you now.

Lord, more often than not, I'm afraid. More often than not I plead with You: *how long?* I become fixated on my fear, on my trouble, on my anxiety and forget entirely about our past together. You've always provided. You've been good to me. Remind me of specific times so that the enemy cannot convince me that I have been forgotten. And worse yet, forgotten by You. Take my broken cries today and turn them into praise. When my patience tires, restore it. And may redemption triumph. Amen.

CHALLENGE

Often our fears and anxieties are birthed from a messy past. Perhaps your childhood wasn't exactly a fairy tale. Or maybe you've been burned, chastised, humiliated. Perhaps you've failed more often than you've won. You can focus on that. You can focus on how you don't feel like God hears you. Or, you can focus on what He's already done for you and through you. And then take that and lean into it hard when you feel like He doesn't hear you. In your journal, write down how God has provided for you. It can be the littlest of things, the smallest of ways. Write it down. Choose to remember.

6

STORMS

A furious squall came up, and the waves broke over the boat, so that it was nearly swamped. Jesus was in the stern, sleeping on a cushion. The disciples woke him and said to him, "Teacher, don't you care if we drown?"
He got up, rebuked the wind and said to the waves, "Quiet! Be still!" Then the wind died down and it was completely calm.
He said to his disciples, "Why are you so afraid? Do you still have no faith?"
They were terrified and asked each other, "Who is this? Even the wind and the waves obey him!"
—Mark 4:37–41

Anxiety can roll in like dark clouds, hovering over our minds, pregnant with troublesome thoughts, alarming assumptions, and premonitions of failure. It quietly blankets our horizon, moving in slowly until we begin to entertain the thoughts, inadvertently turning our faces to the sky and welcoming panic to rain down upon us. Soaking us to the skin.

But anxiety can also swarm us, come upon us like a rapid surge, a crushing blow. Like strong tides, it can sweep us off our feet and out to sea without a moment's notice—before we have time to dig our feet into the sand and hold fast.

I've experienced both. I've fallen victim to both. The tsunami may appear more dangerous, but whether it's a tsunami or a downpour, I always seem to end up in the same place: in the middle of a stormy sea, alone, without a life raft.

As the disciples' boat sliced through calm waters, they too were overcome by a sudden and furious squall. A howling wind ripped through the sails and drew up the waves, like a hurricane effortlessly tugs trees—roots, limbs and all—like pesky weeds from the earth. Drenched to the skin, their sandals soggy with water, the disciples rallied together to hoist the sail, steady the hull, and ride each wave as it crashed over the bow. Grit, sweat, and lake dripped from their faces and swept over their skin. They toiled and tried, experienced seafaring sailors, but even they were no match for the storm's violent blow.

The waves continued to beat against the boat, sending up ominous walls of water that broke over the deck—each threatening to send the men tumbling into the dark sea, forever lost.

The vessel creaked and groaned, the weight of the storm tossing the vessel from side to side like a flimsy plastic bath toy before tipping it toward the heavens and sending it back down to slap against the waters. When the disciples looked up from the task before them, all it took was a quick visual sweep of the boat to know they were in great danger (see Luke 8:23). The vessel, its wooden planks swollen with water, was nearly swamped.

Meanwhile, Jesus slept.

Perhaps exhausted from a day of teaching under the hot sun.[1] Or, perhaps . . . He was waiting.

* * *

Tough, grown men grappled with the rolling waves, trying to control their feeble ship. I wonder how long the storm raged before they woke Jesus.

Regardless, it wasn't until their boat was past saving that they called out. It wasn't until they were nearly swamped that they shook Jesus from His slumber.

> **That's what anxiety looks like as it transcends into the realms of panic and worry: hysteria.**

Rushing to the back of the boat, they began shouting, their words colliding like a symphony of chaos: "Teacher, don't you care if we drown?" (Mark 4:38), "Master, Master, we're going to drown!" (Luke 8:24), "Lord, save us! We're going to drown!" (Matt. 8:25).

Though each Gospel recalls a slightly different combination of words, the sentiment is the same. Each phrase is laced with panic. Each outcry ends in exclamation or doubt. There were a handful of hysterical men on that boat. Death was a real possibility, and Jesus' sleeping was understood to them as disinterest, His quiet, as indifference.

That's what anxiety looks like as it transcends into the realms of panic and worry: hysteria.

So, why is it that we make Jesus our last resort? Why do we wait until the boat is swamped to plea for rescue?

"Jesus, save me!" Your plea emerges like a faint whisper, drowned out by the wind, the chaotic thoughts. Your boat is taking on water.

You're drowning. Perhaps you're drowning right now. Today.

The disciples huddled around Jesus, perhaps shaking Him awake, begging for rescue. Their faces close to His, water dripping from the ends of their noses, each breath heavy with despair.

> **They had more trust in what the *storm* could do than what *Jesus* could do.**

As Jesus woke, He didn't leap to His feet. His eyes didn't grow wide in horror at the size of the storm. He wasn't surprised. No. He stood and with three words rebuked the wind and calmed the waves. *Completely.* "Quiet! Be still!" He said. And at once the storm lifted—leaving as quickly as it came—the waves collapsing into the lake. The winds died down; the waters ceased to boil, no longer even lapping the shoreline. They were still. Entirely still. And a great hush fell over the earth's pool.

Can you imagine the silence? Just the sound of tiny streams of water dripping from the ends of their hair, the railings, and the sails.

And then, from the quiet, Jesus turned to His friends and asked, "Why are you so afraid? Do you still have no faith?"

Faith is the antidote to fear. Prayer, the antidote to worry. The disciples took their trust in Jesus and gave it, though perhaps unintentionally, to the storm around them. They had more trust in what the *storm* could do than what *Jesus* could do. They had faith—it was just misplaced.

Jesus was not sleeping out of carelessness. He did not worry, fret, or feed anxious thoughts. And He was not surprised by the storm. He proved with three little words that everything—every gust of wind, every crashing wave—was under His hand, under His control. Before you journeyed across the ocean over which He called you, He saw the storm that you couldn't have possibly foreseen.

"Be still," He said to the waves. "Be still," in this instance, means to literally muzzle—as if the storm was manic.[2] The phrase sounds familiar, doesn't it? In Psalm 46:10, God says, "Be still, and know that I am God . . ." Be still. But rather than a violent restraining, here the phrase is rooted in the Hebrew word *rāpâ*, which can mean to hang limp, sink down, or be feeble.[3] Like a child who collapses into her father's arms. Yes, this is the quiet our Father desires for us. The storm, the anxiety, requires violent muzzling—*that* is what He wishes to subdue. Not you. You and your anxiety are not one and the same. You are separate. It is not part of who you are. No, anxiety requires active restraint to be still. All you need to do is fall limp into Christ's hands.

Quiet your heart.

Quiet your mind.

Jesus may calm the storm in your soul as He did that day on the Sea of Galilee—or He may ride it out *with* you. Either way, He's in the boat. He was *in* the storm then, and He's *in* your storm now.

So don't entertain anxiousness for a moment. Don't wait to call on Jesus as the disciples did. Muzzle your fear and worry by handing it to the only One who can control it. Because you *can't*—not in your own strength.

The disciples, in sheer amazement at Jesus' miraculous act that day, murmured among themselves, asking, "Who is this? Even the wind and the waves obey him!" A rhetorical question, more or less. For He is the Son of God. And everything that's ever been formed is under His control. All of creation is under His authority.

Don't be stubborn and lean on your own strength. Your strength will crumble like sand beneath you. Instead, rush to the back of your boat and call on Jesus. Don't wait until the storm intensifies and panic is upon you.

Call out as soon as you see the storm clouds rolling in.

Jesus, my heart longs to turn to You first when panic creeps in, but in the midst of the storms in my mind, I often grab tight to something tangible. I rely too much on my own strength. Father, I know You have the power to calm my anxiety. I know You have the means to settle my soul. May You increase my faith and help me fix my eyes on You. Amen.

CHALLENGE

Storms are always brewing. If you're not in the midst of one now, there could be one in next week's forecast. That's life. It's scattered with little landmines set to throw us off course. That's our enemy at work. But we can take practical steps to stay relaxed. This challenge is simple: when a storm starts brewing, brew chamomile tea. While it helps the average person fall asleep, it can help settle an anxious heart. Stash it in the kitchen, put some in your office drawer, and keep a small tin of teabags in your car or purse for when you're on the go.

7

STILL

As Jesus and his disciples were on their way, he came to a village where a woman named Martha opened her home to him. She had a sister called Mary, who sat at the Lord's feet listening to what he said. But Martha was distracted by all the preparations that had to be made. She came to him and asked, "Lord, don't you care that my sister has left me to do the work by myself? Tell her to help me!"
"Martha, Martha," the Lord answered, "you are worried and upset about many things, but only one thing is needed. Mary has chosen what is better, and it will not be taken away from her."
—Luke 10:38–42

The snow came down in torrents, heavy and wet, erasing the color from behind the frosted windowpanes. Dark, bare trees—lifeless—poked through the pillows of white blanketing the landscape.

The small parking lot emptied bit by bit, hour by hour, until no more than a few cars remained.

It was time.

Clutching the crisp linen letter in my hand, I walked into the corner office and closed the door behind me. The tears came quietly, uninvited. No amount of focus or fierce determination could keep them away.

Words seemed meaningless, but they came, though entirely unpolished. This wasn't what I wanted, but my health had taken a nasty turn: sleepless nights, heavy exhaustion, days without food, intense nausea, terrifying nightmares, and routine panic attacks. It had become almost unbearable to leave the house.

That's why I was here, now, in this office. God had asked me to do the unthinkable: deliver my resignation letter.

Everything in me wanted to stay, but God was removing me for reasons I didn't know and couldn't understand at the time. It broke my heart and left me breathless. I blamed myself. I wasn't quitting my job—I was losing it. To a devilish scheme I felt I could no longer fight after months of trying. The brute force within me was simply gone, my fists bloody and bruised. I was still trying to fight in my own strength.

In the eyes of others, the decision to quit my job must have seemed foolish. Unconventional. *Lazy*. I felt as though I was being fired for a catastrophic miscalculation that cost the company and my reputation more than my keep was worth.

I felt—no, I *believed*—I was an utter failure.

As I drove home that evening, ice and snow beating at my windshield, I let out a tired whimper. My throat clenched with tears that threatened to spill over, and my hands shook. I gripped the steering wheel harder. I leaned forward in my seat—away from the pain, away from myself, a little closer to home. The pain was no less than a breakup gone miserably wrong. My heart was in pieces. My dreams, dissolving.

Four weeks later, as I walked out of the building for the last time, there was a quiet sense of relief. One less thing to feed the monster growing inside me. But there was also a sense of tremendous remorse. My pride had taken a major hit. I found my worth, my talent, my significance, my value . . . in my work. In my *doing*.

I had been running toward my goals, not toward His. And He allowed me to pursue those things, to hold tight to a sense of control, knowing it would cost me more than I wanted to give up. In His infinite wisdom, He allowed me to prolong my own suffering because He was, and still is, more concerned with my long-term transformational healing than He is with short-term temporary comfort.

Those of us with a stubborn grip tend to learn the hard way. How much gentler the healing process could have been—would have been—if I had allowed Him to hold my world in His all-powerful hands sooner.

I slept for what felt like days following my departure, my strength eroding with every wave of anxiety. It was still clawing at my skin. A symptom of something far greater.

As my energy came back in small doses, I fetched the basket of cleaning supplies and tore apart the house, cleaning every crevice, organizing every drawer, washing every linen. To numb the guilt, to gain some fraction of control. To get back a sense of worth, of value. Within a week or so, our small townhouse was spotless—the smallest items placed in labeled bins and shirts hung in organized fashion.

Like Martha, I was consumed with everything else but Jesus. Like

Martha, I found my worth in busyness. Like Martha, I found value in my *doing*. And like Martha, I was missing daily encounters with Jesus.

Martha had the gift of hospitality and resourcefulness (see John 12:2). She enjoyed preparing, cleaning, cooking, *doing*. This account in Luke puts her gift in the spotlight. She anxiously went about the house tidying up and, perhaps, preparing a meal for their honored guest and those with Him. Though we aren't told what tasks she attended to, it appears that the more busy she became, the more aware she was of how little two hands could accomplish at once. She began to fret, to worry, about the many preparations.[1]

So she called on Jesus.

"Lord, don't you care that my sister has left me to do the work by myself?" she says. "Tell her to help me!"

Our plea sounds eerily similar: *Lord, don't You see how hard I'm working? Why won't You relieve my anxiety? Why won't You help?*

Martha was doing everything right. And perhaps you are, too. I thought I was. I had a job. A strong career. A healthy paycheck. Society told me to go to college, get good grades, and land a prosperous job. And I did.

It was likely that society told Martha that her role was in the home. She, too, was doing everything right.

So what was the problem?

The problem was being *pulled toward the better* rather than *submitting to the best*.

Jesus saw past Martha's *doing*. Just as He sees past your doing. He cares far more about your state of mind than any task required of you.

In His unique and loving way, Jesus reaches past the anxiousness and speaks directly to Martha's heart. "Martha, Martha," He says. Can you see the kindness in His eyes as He looks upon this frantic woman? Can you hear the intimacy and tenderness in His voice, like a parent speaking with compassion and affection to a young child? He does not condemn Martha's preparations, but shines a bright light into a dark space where anxiety and worry hold her focus. Her anxiousness had distracted her. She had lost sight of what was most important. She was no longer listening. Her busyness had pulled her from the thing of greatest importance: sitting at the feet of Jesus.

Jesus wasn't asking Martha to exchange her gift of hospitality for something else. But for a time, He was asking her to set it aside for a far greater purpose. Jesus did not ask me to exchange my career for therapy. But, for a season, He asked me to set it aside for a greater purpose, a greater calling—to attend to the affairs of my soul.

It didn't seem rational. It didn't seem wise.

Neither did foregoing preparations in Martha's time.

But who are we to question the almighty God?

This story is left suspended in midair. No conclusion, no sequel. We don't know if Martha collapsed at Jesus' feet right then, or if she turned on her heel and huffed and puffed her way back to the kitchen.

We don't know what happened to Martha.

But you can choose what happens to you.

Jesus may be calling you to give something up. To put something aside, temporarily or even permanently. It may be something small. Or it may be something big. He may be asking you to put aside cultural expectations and to embrace *His* expectations and calling on your life. Regardless, He is most certainly beckoning you to be still. To sit at His feet.

> **We don't know what happened to Martha. But you can choose what happens to you.**

Either way, the answer is in Him. Time and time again, we see that the antidote to worry, to anxiousness, to fretting, is to drop everything and kneel at the feet of Jesus. To abide in Him.

So, what will it be? Will you continue doing a two-man job in your strength? Or will you sit and give your full attention to Jesus, putting aside all that is *good*, and embracing all that is *best*?

I can tell you personally . . . it was worth the sacrifice.

Lord, my middle name ought to have been Martha. In my anxiousness, I tend to try to keep busy so I don't have to sit with my thoughts. They're too overwhelming, too frightening. The thought of sitting in the quiet is daunting. Please help me find strength in Mary's example. Help me choose what's best. For nothing will cure my fears but time with You. Help me not to replace You. Remind me to turn to You first in moments of great anxiety. Thank You for never giving up on me. Amen.

CHALLENGE

Take some time today and sit. Just sit. Don't speak. Don't pray. Don't turn on music. Just sit. And wait on the Lord. Close your eyes, lean your head back, point your face to the sun, and be still. Quiet your heart. A quiet heart, a calm soul, is ripe for planting. Allow God to teach you, to speak into your life. Rest in Him. For He longs to hold you.

8

FEAR

The LORD said to Gideon, "You have too many men for me to deliver Midian into their hands. In order that Israel may not boast against me that her own strength has saved her, announce now to the people, 'Anyone who trembles with fear may turn back and leave Mount Gilead.'" So twenty-two thousand men left, while ten thousand remained.
—Judges 7:2–3

The cursor blinked ominously against the stark white page. Blank, waiting to be filled. But nothing came. Nothing spilled out. I was so full of words, yet they were stuck somewhere between my brain and my fingertips. I leaned forward and lightly touched the keys. A sentence came, but the words read empty. They didn't hold the weight of what my heart desperately wanted to communicate.

I held the backspace key.

And there it was again: the empty page. The mocking hum of the computer—it droned on and on just like my negative thoughts. Relentless.

I can't do this.

I slammed the lid of laptop shut. Or rather, *fear* slammed it. Fear of failure. Fear of judgment. Fear of unintentionally breaking the rules and getting it all wrong. The fear of empty words filling meaningless pages.

Fear stopped me that day. And the next. Until days rolled into weeks, into months, into years. Years of silence. Years of words caught up tight in my throat. They kept me from breathing, living, as God intended. This pent-up emotion intending to be spilled onto pages, yet resistance overcoming it.

He put me on this path, this journey, and out of fear and worry, I trembled and balked at the thought of being used for the kingdom. That's the enemy's goal, right? He can't have our souls, so he'll do everything in his power to make us inefficient while we're here. I began to question: was I called? Surely not. Surely God intended to use someone else. Someone more skilled, more stable, more worthy and gifted. So I did as any fool would do and assessed God's intent and purpose for my words with my feeble human reasoning. My assessment revealed that it was best to silence those words. To put an end to the so-called purpose that was certainly an invention conjured up in my mind.

But the urge never ceased. My fingers burned to write. They bled. My mind was consumed with thoughts that could not possibly have come from an anxious heart, for they were keys to unlocking freedom from it. They could have come only from a Savior. And yet, as soon as I went to put fingers to keypad or pen to paper, anxiety would seize my heart, and I would succumb to it. I hardly put up a fight.

Anxiety is a powerful emotion. So powerful that if you allow anxious thoughts to turn into worried actions, you'll become unproductive for the kingdom. Satan will do his best to steamroll you with doubt, stall you, create detours, and convince you the path God set for you is impassible. And if he can convince you of this, you'll be nothing but a broken tool in the hands of a mighty God.

When Gideon was called to lead the Israelites, he was not addressed by his name, but rather by his intended purpose. "The LORD is with you, mighty warrior," the angel said (Judg. 6:12).

> **And if he can convince you of this, you'll be nothing but a broken tool in the hands of a mighty God.**

Although Gideon resisted at first, the Lord was patient. And Gideon soon humbled himself to the Lord's plan—comforted, I'm sure, by the fact that he wasn't about to deliver the Israelites alone. For God said, "I will be with you, and you will strike down all the Midianites together" (Judg. 6:16). The great strike was not to glorify Gideon or the Israelites; it was to glorify God.

How terrifying it must have been for Gideon that when his troops gathered at the spring of Harod, God's first words to him as leader were, "You have too many men for me to deliver Midian into their hands." Too many? Gideon had 32,000 men to the enemy's 135,000.[1] Surely God didn't mean to reduce their numbers. It was illogical. Unreasonable. Scatterbrained. Senseless. But God knew that even at 32,000, the Israelites could boast that victory came by their own strength.

So how did God choose who would fight for Him? By first removing those who were *afraid.*

Fear has a particular stench. It permeates a room; others can sense it. It's contagious, too.[2] Deuteronomy 20:8 says, "Then the officers shall add, 'Is any man afraid or fainthearted? Let him go home so that his brothers will not become disheartened too.'" Yes, it is mightily contagious. So He sent the fearful home.

How many anxious hearts bent toward worry and fear have sacrificed their role in a great movement of God?

Twenty-two thousand of the 32,000 turned back. More than two thirds of Gideon's army journeyed down the mountain that day and returned home.

Had they not been afraid, perhaps they would have been part of God's miraculous delivery. But they were not leaning on God and His strength—they were relying on their own. And that was not pleasing to God. So He set them aside and focused on the 10,000 who were not trembling in fear. He narrowed that bunch down, too. But what struck me most was that those who feared were removed first. And how *many* there were.

How many anxious hearts bent toward worry and fear have sacrificed their role in a great movement of God? How many have turned their backs and walked down the mountain? How many have been called by God not by name, but by *purpose*, and have used every excuse not to follow through on His calling.

How does the Lord whisper to you? Does He call you mighty warrior as He did Gideon? Or does He call you selfless teacher, gifted writer, powerful speaker, loving mother, courageous student? What has He called you to? What dream of God's have you allowed fear to snuff out?

You may desire an ordinary life with ordinary things and ordinary plans. But God has extraordinary plans for His children if only they would listen to His calling on their lives. And the enemy will do everything in his power to prevent it from unfolding. Remember: He knows he cannot have your soul, so he will cripple you in ways you never knew possible. He will get you to question yourself, your value, your worth. He'll find a foothold in your mind—play games with your head. Anything to prevent you from following the call on your life.

So fight. May we press on so that we are not removed from God's army. So that we can be one of the few whom God can use to bring glory to Himself. What an honor, truly.

But will worry rob you of your purpose? Will you allow it to stall you? Or will you stand and fight?

This is a call to arms.

Father, You used Gideon and Moses and Noah and many others like them. You used the least of these to glorify Your name. You used the weak, the young, the old. Your eyes roam the earth looking for open hearts. May my heart be one of them. May the calling on my life be clear. May fear not cloud Your dreams for me. I don't want my fear or worry to be contagious; I want my love for You to be contagious. I surrender my worry to You once again, Lord. And pray that the days ahead will give me the tools to fight my fear. Amen.

CHALLENGE

What is fear robbing you of? Write it down in your journal today. Does fear rob you of friendships? Does it keep you from venturing out of your home? Does it prevent you from applying for that job for fear of rejection? Does your relationship with your spouse suffer? Write down each one and keep it close by. It'll be your ammunition—the very reasons you'll choose to stay with the army and fight—in the days ahead.

9

RESOLVE

*Alarmed, Jehoshaphat resolved to inquire of the Lord, and he
proclaimed a fast for all of Judah . . .
"For we have no power to face this vast army that is attacking us.
We do not know what to do, but our eyes are upon you."*
—2 Chronicles 20:3, 12

When my husband asked for my hand in marriage, the answer
was a tearful, barely audible, yet obnoxiously high-pitched, "yes."
"No" didn't have a fraction of a second to enter my thoughts. When
given the choice between chocolate and vanilla, the answer is
always vanilla. A cup of tea or a cup of coffee? It's hardly a question, for nothing warms my soul the way a mug of silky java does.

Some decisions come without an ounce of hesitation. There may
be no wrong, no right, only personal preference—taste buds, even.

Other decisions come with a side of consequence, sacrifice. There's
risk involved. Like a fork in the road, both paths look well-worn.
Both paths seem logical—a smart choice. Yet, one path leads
to prosperity and joy: God's will for your life. The other, while
appearing just as profitable and opportunistic, may be marred by
regret and trouble somewhere down the road. *Take this job offer*

or wait for something else? Move or settle down here? Quit or stay? Start a family or wait? Go to college or get a job? Stay together or break up? The deeper questions, the heavier decisions: those are the ones that keep us awake at night. They claw at our minds. They're decisions you feel you can't make, ones you can't resolve.

Nothing can stir up worry in an anxious heart quite like decision making.

When a decision is demanded, I turn to my husband, call my mom, or ask a colleague for his or her advice. I lean in hard. I pay close attention to each word, to each syllable of wisdom. I keep quiet and give them the floor. My pastor advises, my friend empathizes, and all the while, my Bible collects dust. The answer is right there on my nightstand, but I instead choose to vent to my best friend, talk to the cat or, more often than not, to myself.

> **Nothing can stir up worry in an anxious heart quite like decision making.**

Jehoshaphat, a wise and godly king who walked with the Lord (see 2 Chron. 17:5–6), had a decision to make as well. Soon after reforming his kingdom, the king received word that the Moabites and Ammonites, along with some of the Meunites, were coming upon his city to make war. By the time the intelligence got to Jehoshaphat, they had already trespassed into his country.[1]

Worse yet, there was no apparent reason for the attack.[2] Isn't that so even in our own lives? Conflict, heartache, and chaos strike with little, if any, warning.

The king, hearing this news, was "alarmed." He was frightened, and naturally so. After all, anxiety is not sinful; it is an emotion, a feeling very similar to anger. We can have righteous anger toward abuse, neglect, starvation, and similar injustices. In fact, those things ought to anger us because it spurs us on to godly action. Anger becomes sin when those clenched fists lash out and strike a loved one. Or when cursing seeps from our lips like wet heat from our brow. That is sin. The emotion itself is simply a state of consciousness, a reflex. It makes us human.

King Jehoshaphat was at a crossroads. Immediately upon hearing the news, his heart sank, the hair on the back of his neck stood erect, and his hands trembled. He was anxious. Frightened. He could have decided in that moment to sit upon his throne and ponder all the ways in which his kingdom would be upturned. He could have trembled in fear while his people crumbled under his lack of leadership. He could have called his attendants and those in leadership roles and weighed the opinion of each. That was one option, one path.

He chose an alternative.

I once heard bestselling author Lysa TerKeurst speak, and loved when she pointed out in Scripture that Jehoshaphat's name is sandwiched between two words, "alarmed" and "resolved." He was alarmed, an emotional reaction to a very real threat. He could have sat down and worried, but he didn't. His anxiousness propelled him to immediately inquire of the Lord.[3]

Jehoshaphat was a wise man. He knew his hope rested in God. He knew the decision he made next should be God-lead and God-directed. Without God, his people would be crushed beneath the weight of an army that was far more prepared than his own.

And so he inquires of the Lord and proclaimed a fast for all of Judah. They came together with one purpose, under one King—the True King—to seek direction. And Jehoshaphat humbled himself and stood before the assembly and prayed. What strikes me is the close of his prayer, "For we have no power to face this vast army that is attacking us. We do not know what to do, but our eyes are upon you" (2 Chron. 20:12). And then all of Judah, the young and the old, the men and their wives and children, stood and waited for God.

I hear Jehoshaphat's prayer echoed in my own: "God, I don't know what to do." But how often do I wait on Him? As the men, women, and children stood before God in the temple, the army against them continued marching toward their city. Every moment of inaction counted. Every second, precious.

We don't know how much time passed; the crowd may have stood before the Lord for minutes, even hours. Regardless, they waited. They stood together, anticipating a response to their need and were faithful to wait patiently until the Spirit of the Lord came upon someone in the assembly who said: "Listen, King Jehoshaphat and all who live in Judah and Jerusalem! This is what the LORD says to you: 'Do not be afraid or discouraged because of this vast army. For the battle is not yours, but God's'" (20:15).

Friend, this battle is not your own. We are called to be obedient to Christ, and God will carry out the rest.[4]

Easier said than done, no?

The declaration in verse 15 was then followed by specific instructions and one more reminder not to be afraid: "Go out to face them tomorrow, and the LORD will be with you" (20:17).

The next morning, as they prepared for battle, a select few whom Jehoshaphat appointed led the men forward with song and praise to the Lord. They led the others, saying, "Give thanks to the LORD for his love endures forever" (20:21). They entered the battle with thanksgiving and praise *even though* they didn't know what was before them. *Even though* the battle plan wasn't crystal clear. God did not reveal every detail of His plan, but asked them to move forward in faith, obeying the few instructions He gave.

They did, and as they marched forward in obedience, sending praises heavenward, God fulfilled His promise.

By the time they crested the hill that overlooked the desert, the vast army they feared was no longer a threat. The men were dead. The Lord had caused them to turn on each other, and they slaughtered one another. Jehoshaphat and his men did not need to raise a sword or even charge down the hill. It was taken care of before they arrived to the battle.

Resolve to pray. Resolve to lift your hands in worship, and perhaps you will not have to lift your hands in battle.

The decisions that require your attention and often breed worry may seem like a vast army before you. But remember this: God is never late, and, despite our wishes, He is rarely early. He arrives at just the appointed time. The perfect time.

When we become alarmed at life's curveballs, which are bound to come, may we resolve to lift our eyes to Christ and inquire of the Lord as Jehoshaphat did. There is no other way to lead your life, let alone the lives God may have entrusted to you: your children, your spouse.

It's so easy to say "Yes, I will resolve to inquire of the Lord," and far more difficult to follow through. But I beg you to try. Resolve to pray. Resolve to lift your hands in worship, and perhaps you will not have to lift your hands in battle. For the battle will have been won before you even get there—wherever "there" may be.

You are a child of the Most High. A daughter or son of the living King. Press into Him with prayer and thanksgiving. Present your requests, your anxieties, your fears, your troubles, and your conflicts to God. He is with you. He is *for* you.

Father, decisions abound in my life. Some decisions come easy. Others, not so much. Sometimes I become so overwhelmed at making the wrong decision that I turn to the tangible—the people I can see—to make those choices for me. Help me resolve to turn to You in the midst of my alarm. For You are good and You are strong and the battle is Yours. Help me trust You with it. Amen.

CHALLENGE

Resolving to turn to Jesus requires surrendering your will, which is a daily giving up and letting go. It can take some hand-holding, a gentle prodding from someone else. May I be your "someone else" today?

Resolve to surrender today's decisions and commit them to prayer. This takes practice before becoming habit. But today, I encourage you to stand in confidence before God as Jehoshaphat did, and *wait* for Him to speak into your life. Wait expectantly. Tomorrow, may you resolve to do it again. But for now, just focus on today, for today will require enough strength.

10

RETRAIN

We demolish arguments and every pretension that sets itself up against the knowledge of God, and we take captive every thought to make it obedient to Christ.
—2 Corinthians 10:5

and do not give the devil a foothold.
—Ephesians 4:27

He looked me square in the face, eyebrows arched, hands moving back and forth, and explained anxiety as forming pathways in the brain. When fears arise—rational or irrational—our brains direct those fears down neural pathways, he said. Everything we've ever learned has carved a path in the brain. The way we've repeatedly coped with our anxieties and fears has essentially created worried pathways over time. We've essentially *taught* our minds to worry. Medication helps to "reroute" these paths temporarily. Like guardrails, medication helps keep our thoughts on the highway, so to speak, as opposed to the rural back roads littered with potholes and traps.

While our thoughts are "rerouted," we can practice new strategies and techniques, which will ultimately retrain our brains. But we must practice them repetitively to make progress, to make new neural associations.

It was as though I had just read the abbreviated version of Brain Chemistry 101.

He put his hands on his knees and then patted mine. "You're just an anxious person," he said sweetly, drawing an encouraging smile across his face. "Just think of it as part of your charm."

I stood and walked out the door with two low-dose prescriptions in hand.

And it was the best thing I could have done for myself.

You may be surprised to hear me say that, as many often are. But psychological woes can be just as debilitating as physical ailments. Just as a diabetic needs insulin, so an anxious person may need medication. I would not deny a diabetic insulin and therefore should not deny myself the balm to soothe my mental strain while I work on getting rid of Satan's foothold in my mind. It is just one aspect of a treatment *regime.*

Hence why I didn't *just* walk out of that office with two prescriptions that day. I walked out with a burning determination and a fierce resolve.

"You're just an anxious person," he had said. "It's part of your charm." Those were words, though they'd taken on various forms, that had been spoken over my life for years. Whether it was disguised as a compliment (*You're a perfectionist.*) or a dig (*You can't let anything go!*), it all boiled down to anxiety. And I realized, in that moment, that I could choose to wear a label that read, "Hi, my name is Anxious," or I could fight. I could make changes. I could retrain—rewire—my brain.

Occasionally, someone who requires prescription medication can make life changes to improve his or her health. I have heard countless testimonies of men and women putting their pills aside after working hard to regain overall wellness. It's not the same for everyone. Certainly there are physical and psychological ailments that are irreversible. But I resolve to fight.

I could choose to wear a label that read, "Hi, my name is Anxious," or I could fight.

Perhaps, like me, you are prone to anxiousness. You have a Type-A personality, lust after perfection and flawlessness, and are characterized by your work ethic, productivity, and competitiveness. These are characteristics to be proud of. But like any good thing, it must be practiced in moderation. When you don't know how to rein those qualities in, you end up like me: a victim. Enslaved to your thoughts. A captive in your own skin.

God didn't design you that way. He doesn't create "worriers," because He can't create something that violates His Word. Your organizational flair, resourcefulness, productivity . . . those characteristics are part of your charm, my charm. But somewhere along the way, those things that worked for us and made us unique morphed into something ugly and turned against us. That's why it's so important to take each and every thought captive and make it obedient to Christ.

God does not intend for us to live in anxiety. He intends for us to live abundantly. To taste His glory, enjoy His creation, and harness the fullness of life.

We may be wrapped up a little tighter than most. We may have to think proactively to avoid worry. But I want to live in freedom. I want a life free from worry. From fear. From self-condemnation. I want to live as Christ. To face the anxiousness with feet planted strong and come through victorious. Don't you?

My name is Samantha—not Anxious. And I'm child of the King. I may have a *tendency* toward anxiousness, but I refuse to be defined by it. I choose to live in, and fight for, freedom in Christ. And I *will* fight. And fight hard so that the enemy may not gain a foothold in my mind and turn this disciple into a paralyzed prisoner. Shackled in my own fear, entirely ineffective for the kingdom. What about you? What's *your* name? Place your name into this paragraph, and read it again.

Let's watch our giant buckle at the knees before the evidence of the power of Jesus Christ at work in our lives.

As I write, I'm on this journey with you. I, too, am learning how to fight. I've walked with you, in part, through the trembling. These last ten days, we've held hands and gently meandered down this narrow road. We've surrendered daily, together. You've met small challenges and simple tasks. Challenges I've completed as well.

This is now a call to arms. A call to engage in a spiritual battle that has only just begun. To put on the armor of Christ and engage in hand-to-hand combat with the enemy—an enemy who wants nothing more than to crush you with worry and fear. Are you watchful? Are you guarding yourself against the enemy's lies?

Are you winning?

Join me. Join me in a crusade against the giant. Let's watch our giant buckle at the knees before the evidence of the power of Jesus Christ at work in our lives. Let's learn to live an abundant life, the one Jesus won for us on the cross.

Heavenly Father, remind me that Your name for me is not Anxious. It's not Worry Wart. It's not Fearful. It's My Child. Only by Your strength and supernatural power will I be able to overcome my anxiety and take captive each thought. Help me remember that through the power of the Holy Spirit, I am able because You are able. On those days of struggle, remind me that my anxious thoughts and worried behaviors do not define who I am in You. For You have delivered me. You have paid the price. Help me rest in my identity in You. Amen.

CHALLENGE

I need you to find another sticky note. This time, I want you to write: "I am a daughter/son of the Most High King." Tape it to the mirror. You must begin redefining who you are to yourself. You must retrain your brain and reroute your thoughts. Repeat the words "I am a daughter/son of the Most High King" each morning. Because the battles will come. Anxiousness will tempt you. *The choice to worry or to worship will be before us nearly every day.* Who are you? You are a child of God. And through Him you have the power to conquer each and every anxious thought.

Take the thoughts captive before they take *you* captive.

fight

FRAGILE

11

GOLIATH

A champion named Goliath, who was from Gath, came out of the Philistine camp. He was over nine feet tall. He had a bronze helmet on his head and wore a coat of scale armor of bronze weighing five thousand shekels; on his legs he wore bronze greaves, and a bronze javelin was slung on his back. His spear shaft was like a weaver's rod, and its iron point weighed six hundred shekles. His shield bearer went ahead of him.
—1 Samuel 17:4–7

There he is. Brazen and brutish, emerging from the place where all your burdens and secret fears camp. He stands tall, off in the distance. Looming, stalking. You didn't coax him from his tent. You didn't invite him; rather, you resolved a long time ago to keep a great distance from him. Though a deep valley, like a battle line, lies between your camp and his, he still comes forward like a towering fortress.

He's your Goliath.

*   *   *

The Israelites had driven out the Philistine army nearly three centuries ago. But with Saul weak and unfit, having been forsaken by Samuel, it was a perfect opportunity for the enemy to take revenge.

So they put forward their very best: a man named Goliath, a champion. He stood over nine feet tall—by some accounts, nearly eleven.[1] His helmet was made of bronze. His coat was crafted of brass plates—scales, like feathers kicking out, covered his chest, his rippling shoulders and arms on display. Goliath's shoes, like shin-guards, were made of bronze, and he carried a bronze javelin across his back.[2] The tip of his spear, made from solid iron, weighed 15 pounds. His coat alone weighed a hefty 125 pounds—as much as a young man. A man like David.[3]

And if that wasn't enough, a shield bearer went ahead of him—a second line of defense.

That is how Goliath emerged from his camp. Each step jostled his heavy armor. The ominous *shink, shink, shink* echoed across the valley, as if to prove without words how weak and insignificant the Israelites were.

They didn't stand a chance.

Every detail was known about this behemoth, and the writer of this passage spends a good deal of time describing him. The focus: the enemy's appearance. He was a champion, after all. A fighter. Surely the Israelite army had studied his history, his preferred method of attack. And quite naturally, they were terrified. The Israelites were fixated by the tremendous boom of his voice. His taunting and jeering. This wasn't just a man—this was a monster. Any man sent out to fight him would surely be crushed beneath his iron fist, leaving their remaining comrades enslaved to the enemy (1 Sam. 17:9). It was a suicide mission.

As Max Lucado points out in his book *Facing Your Giants*, the Israelites saw only *Goliath*: "A subplot appears in the story. More than 'David versus Goliath,' this is 'God-focus versus giant-focus.'"4 And for days they sat atop their hill, the enemy on theirs, and the two just looked at each other.

How long have you stared at your giant—your anxieties—willing them to go away? How much time and thought have you spent sizing up your enemy, your "what ifs"? How many times have you fled in panic at the mere sound of his jostling armor?

Your giant may not carry a spear or stand cloaked in metal and brass, but he may as well be. Your giant, like mine, is worry. He wakes you with troubling thoughts, stirs stress beneath your skin, and consumes your mind with fear. He breathes down your neck, hot and wet, making you squirm. It's as if he plants anxious thoughts into your mind that slowly—and sometimes swiftly—propel you into the arms of worry, causing you to behave in ways that grieve the heart of your Savior. Not because He's disappointed with you, but because it hurts to see you in bondage.

Remember, anxiety is an *emotion*. Worry is a *behavior*. This is such a critical distinction; I desperately want you to take hold of that truth. Anxiety, like anger, is nothing more than a feeling. Jesus felt the pounding of an anxious heart before He was arrested. He grieved over the loss of Lazarus. And anger lit a fire under His skin over the misuse of His Father's house (see Luke 22:44; John 11:33; and John 2:13–16). While not pleasant emotions, they are still only emotions.

However, emotions or feelings are catalysts to behavior, which can result in sin.

When you are anxious, you can choose to dwell in the birthplace of the tormenting thoughts. You can sit with them awhile, invite them in, have them spend the night, and allow those thoughts to dictate your day and dominate your tomorrow.

Or, you can pray, as Jesus did, without ceasing. Like an arm stretched taunt toward the heavens. Until you have the strength to stand on your feet once more and leave your anxiety at the foot of the cross. Jesus could have given into worry that night in the Garden of Gethsemane. In the temple, He could have given into rage, cursing and throwing His fists into the faces of the peddlers. He did neither. Had He, His sacrifice on the cross would have been nothing more than a brutal execution.

Know your giant. Study your Goliath. But *see* **(blepō) your God.**

The Israelites lent their eyes to sizing up their giant. They spent considerable time studying him. And while this is a wise battle strategy, they took God out of the equation. In the same way Peter *saw* (blepō) the wind, we could suggest that the Israelites *saw* (blepō) the enemy. They were fixated, taken, overwhelmed. Fear held their gaze steadfast. And, as a result, they didn't see their God. *Couldn't* see their God. They were facing the wrong direction.

Size up your Goliath. Study his habits. What triggers his voice? Does he pilfer your sleep? Run you ragged at work? When does he provoke you with negative, demeaning, self-defeating thoughts? What triggers his relentless taunting? Know him. Know your Goliath.

But put him in his proper place: side by side with the living God. Then, and only then, will you see how small your Goliath is compared to your Heavenly Father and have the courage to climb down your hill and across the battle line. Let me be frank: you don't have the strength to overcome worry.

But God does.

Know your giant. Study your Goliath. But *see* (blepō) your God.

Heavenly Father, my Goliath is catastrophically huge. He appears insurmountable. He threatens defeat each day. To be honest, I do my best to avoid him—and I don't dare fight him. I am terrified I will fail and succumb to his crushing blows. That he will become more relentless if I give him even the slightest attention. I figure if I ignore him enough, he'll go away. Help me keep my eyes fixed on You. Help me see my Goliath, but *see* You, my Savior, my Redeemer before me. I need to know my enemy in order to fight him. But as I study my Goliath's tactics and battle plans, remind me to compare him not to my own strength, but to Yours. I know that then, and only then, will he flee in retreat. Amen.

CHALLENGE

Be self-aware today. Set up mental checkpoints throughout your day to evaluate your thoughts. If you begin to feel anxious, do your best to pause and observe. What occurred to cause this overwhelming feeling? Consciously focus on taking deep breaths through your nose and out your mouth. Take an inventory of your thoughts, and pray. Keep track of your Goliath's comings and goings. Write them down. Keep a log. *Don't give him the luxury of sneaking up behind you.* Study him, know him, and verbally remind worry of its place before the throne of grace.

12

STAND

*Goliath stood and shouted to the ranks of Israel, "Why do you
come out and line up for battle? Am I not a Philistine, and are
you not the servants of Saul? Choose a man and have him come
down to me. If he is able to fight and kill me, we will become your
subjects; but if I overcome him and kill him, you will become our
subjects and serve us." Then the Philistine said, "This day I defy
the ranks of Israel! Give me a man and let us fight each other."
On hearing the Philistine's words, Saul and all the Israelites were
dismayed and terrified.*
—1 Samuel 17:8–11

Why do you even bother trying?

You're going to fail.

You're unqualified, untrained, and unfit for the task before you.

Your Goliath's words echo across the valley, pregnant with obscene
lies and taunting sneers. Those words, like venom spewed, seep
deep into the pores of your skin. Rather than reject them, you
choose to absorb them, allowing them to seep deeper, deeper into
your soul. You dwell on these words, perhaps even convincing

yourself that there's a bit of truth within them—though they are void of truth altogether. Brainwashed by these relentless, far-away taunts, you allow the words—those that once resided only in your mind—to roll subtly from your tongue. You have been infected, believing each self-defeating, knit-together phrase, and now speak them into your own life.

And there you have it. Goliath has won before lifting a finger. His words have pinned you in place, paralyzing you with fear. The words turn to thought and then to action: worry. And if you keep up this revolving, ever-turning cycle, you'll have defined your destiny, though you admittedly never intended to.

Your Goliath stands up and shouts each day, doesn't he? Though you stand with an army of angels behind you, the enemy does not appear threatened. He will do everything in his power to convince you that you're power*less*.

The Israelites were dismayed, terrified, by the words of *one* man.

Words are powerful. Proverbs 18:21 says, "Death and life are in the power of the tongue" (ESV). Death and life. No middle ground. My pastor once said, "If you want to change your life, change the words you speak." Not just to others—but the words you speak to yourself. In your mind. In your heart.

When your Goliath rises with the sun, positive thinking mustered up from your battered heart will not send him cowering back into the hole from which he came. However, repeating the words of Jesus Christ will give the enemy no place to stand.

Isn't it strange, though, that when we stand toe-to-toe with our Goliath, we forget every promise, every hope there is in Christ? The Israelites reacted the same way. "On hearing the Philistine's words, Saul and all the Israelites were dismayed and terrified" (1 Sam. 17:11). The word *dismayed* can literally mean "to be shattered."[1] I cannot think of a more accurate description of how worry destroys. When the taunting words from your Goliath spew, it's as if the glass walls surrounding you shatter in agonizing slow motion—rivets snapping, glass erupting. Shards of glass slicing at your feeble strength.

And you retreat in a desperate attempt to silence his verbal blows.

But what if you didn't retreat as the Israelites did? What if you courageously ducked beneath the words and clung to the promises of the God of the universe? And what does He promise?

That He will never leave you or forsake you (Deut. 31:8).

That the battle is His and His alone (1 Sam. 17:47).

That He will sustain you (Ps. 55:22).

That He cares for you (1 Pet. 5:7).

Why do we forget these things when we need them most? The Israelites neglected the promises of God, too, and leaned instead on their ailing, earthly king. They lost their faith in the covenant promises of the Lord and sought security in a human instead.[2] Foolish. Troubling. Yet, we do this every day, relying on the strength of our flesh rather than in the promises of our Savior.

The Israelites faced a valley of death, quite literally. Crippling worry and panic can feel like a valley of death, too. Perhaps you've resided there for years, even decades. You believe there is no way beyond the hills that flank the edges of the lowlands.

But there is. If you choose to fight. If you choose to cross that battle line. When you stand face-to-face with the rival team, do you resign? Of course not! You give it all you have until the clock runs out.

Resolve today not to retreat. Stand. Stand before the fears that stare you down. Stand before your Goliath. Stand, and as the taunts and lies fly like burning arrows toward your side

Just stand. And remember: the battle is His.

of the battlefield, take up the shield of faith. Draw up the promises of Jesus Christ—the sword of the Spirit—to the forefront of your mind (Eph. 6:16–17).

And continue to stand. Just stand. And remember: the battle is His.

Lord, help me to stand strong before my Goliath. Hold me fast so I don't retreat into my corner. Help me not to lose my place in the battle. Remind me of who You are and who I am *in* You. This battle *will* be won, and I will stand on Your promises. This day and the days to come. Amen.

CHALLENGE

You cannot stand on His promises without knowing His promises. In your journal, spend time writing down the truth. Write down the verses I've listed above and add them to the list. Abide in the Word. Arming yourself with the Truth, surrounding yourself with His promises, and leaning into Christ are the only hopes you have in slaying your giant.

13

GAMES

*For forty days the Philistine came forward every morning and
evening and took his stand.*
—1 Samuel 17:16

Worry enjoys the early morning and the close of the day—when all is quiet and undisturbed and distractions are few.

Worry is relentless. Even when you think you've silenced the giant, he returns unscathed. He's consistent, too, never missing a beat. Every morning, every evening, he rises strong. And you cower beneath him—his venomous stench making it hard to find air. You can't even muster the strength to pray him away. You open your mouth and . . . nothing. A dry emptiness.

Worry enjoys the early morning and the close of the day—when all is quiet and undisturbed and distractions are few. That's when he makes his stand. Those times when he is most likely to be heard. When our days are just beginning, hot water pouring over our faces and down our backs, he influences our thoughts, tempting us to turn them towards the day's "what ifs." At night, as we pull the blankets over our heavy shoulders, he sneaks in and robs our sleep. And when we eventually do succumb to heavy eyelids, it's as if he attacks our dreams instead, rehashing our day and convincing us that all went wrong. Even if it isn't so.

Goliath took a stand for forty days, spewing lies and hurling mockery—playing mind games with the Truth. Forty: it's a number that shows up often throughout Scripture and is usually associated with testing, trial, or judgment.[1] Jesus was tempted by the devil during his forty-day fast in the desert. The Israelites wandered around for forty years. And Noah watched the rain fall for forty days and forty nights (see Matt. 4:1–11; Josh. 5:6; and Gen. 7:12).

> **God's plan for our lives is always greater than the one the enemy convinces us to believe in.**

Goliath took his stand for forty *days*—but David, just a mere shepherd boy, would one day reign as king for forty *years* (see 2 Sam. 5:4).

That's one way to stick it to the enemy.

God's plan for our lives is always greater than the one the enemy convinces us to believe in.

Everyone has a trigger. An event, an episode, a word, a task . . . something . . . that causes your Goliath to stand up tall. For me, he rises during the 9-to-5 work day. As a writer and, at times, a proofreader, worry convinces me that I'll miss a comma, a hyphen, a period, or make a catastrophic mistake that will send my employer spiraling into financial failure. As I sit up in bed, I must choose then to surrender my day. But I often forget—rushing through the morning, making lunches, guzzling coffee, and applying the mask of bravery.

As I walk through those big glass doors, or put my fingers to the keyboard, my giant hovers over me like a shadow, mocking me. Convincing me of failure before a flaw is ever detected. Convincing me that success is defined as perfection. One mistake always overshadows a thousand victories. And in panic, I check. I check what I've written one, two, ten times. I proofread once and then again and again and again. And as I hand in an assignment, I rush back and check it once more. Like an itch, I compulsively check and double-check, turning what should have been a five-minute task into one-hour uphill battle.

I make it through the day, my brain deflated from mental strain, and drive home. And as the night falls and darkness consumes the day, doubt blankets my thoughts. *Did I check that? Is that grammatically correct? What if I made a mistake? What if I let them down? What if . . .* And the wretched cycle continues. Like the Israelites, I often flee rather than fight. I scurry to the bedroom in fear, distract myself with a novel, busy myself with household chores, or plant myself in front of the television.

And because I didn't take every thought captive, it spiraled out of control.

I don't know why I check. But my theory is this: I have rules about what is good and right, and what is bad and wrong. Creating my own set of Ten Commandments is just one of many desperate attempts to control some aspect of my life—any aspect. Often, the rules are innocent, but over time, they warp into strange self-torture mechanisms. It's the long and short of why I suffered for several years from an eating disorder, the root of which was founded in severe anxiety. It started as an innocent diet. The thought: *I should be more aware of what I eat.* But over time, my healthy thoughts turned into unhealthy thoughts.

And because I didn't take every thought captive, it spiraled out of control. The rules surrounding my calorie count became irrational, the number on the scale was always wrong, certain foods were no longer allowed. Ultimately, those self-inflicted rules guided me down a path of disillusionment and shame.

I tremble at life's gray moments. I walk around them, avoid them, preferring instead to chase black and white. I prefer to believe that life comes with rules. Yes and no. Good and bad. Right and wrong. Without them, I erupt into internal chaos. Without rules, I have nothing to measure up to, nothing to determine if I'm doing well *enough*. If I'm good *enough*.

Whenever I chose to fight one stronghold in my life, Goliath convinced me to take control of something else. Worry convinced me that I needed control when God was pleading with me to turn it over to Him. But when worry rises with you in the morning and reminds you of its presence at nightfall, it's hard to believe anything but its threats. Your Goliath—the temptation to worry—is relentless.

> **But like self-inflicted *rules*, rules written with your own hand, they often result in self-inflicted *wounds*.**

As a stubborn fool, I rested—and continue to do so at times—on my own strength. But when we worry and idolize our self-inflicted rules, we ultimately put faith in ourselves and deny God our trust.

If you have a Goliath named Worry camping out in your backyard, I believe you may have self-inflicted rules, too. You've created a list of "rules" in your mind that determine success or failure. They are standards that very few, if anyone, can measure up to. When you break one of your rules, failure swallows you whole. The irony is that you feel prisoner—slave—to those rules. But like self-inflicted *rules*, rules written with your own hand, they often result in self-inflicted *wounds*. And worse yet, you've created a belief system that you've trained your mind to live by.

And those rules are nothing more than lies straight from the lips of the enemy:

Don't get an A on the test? You're stupid.

Don't get the promotion or the account? You're a failure.

Don't wash your hands ten times? You'll contract a deadly illness.

Don't have dinner on the table by six o'clock? He'll find a better wife.

Lose your cool with the kids? You're the worst parent ever.

Sexually abused as a child? You're damaged goods.

No one told you these were the rules by which to live. Fear—fear of failure, fear of mistakes, fear of something—delivered the rules into your hands, and you closed your fist around them. You may have resisted at first, but as the lies grew louder and stronger and more consistent, you accepted them. It's tantamount to mind wrestling. Your giant convinces you that if you don't worry, you won't be prepared. If you aren't prepared, you'll fail. And if you fail, you'll never be good at anything at all. If you don't worry about the future, the future will have its way with you. If you don't worry about your kids, you're a bad parent.

So your worry says.

For forty days Goliath's taunts echoed across the valley. The Israelites didn't even bother drawing close to the battle line. They remained posted, but never engaged. While they sat stagnant, Goliath grew more confident, bolder. He got cocky.

Each one of us has, at some point, become lazy in our response to our giant. But backing down every day? There's no excuse in that. Goliath grew stronger as a result of the Israelites' inaction. The more that they tolerated his presence, the more he shamed them. It is only logical to assume that the Israelites became more and more disheartened and fearful the longer they left Goliath's challenge unanswered.

Remember the days before worry? When did you stop fighting and start closing your fingers around the lies, holding them tight to your chest? How many weeks have you spent listening to his repetitive lines? How many months? How many years? When did they become self-inflicted rules? Surely it's been longer than forty days. How long have you sat on your hill, hoping worry will give up and move on?

I've got news for you: he won't. You have to fight. It's a mind game. A battle for your thoughts. You, child of God, were not given a spirit of fear, "but of power, and of love, and of a *sound mind*" (2 Tim. 1:7, KJV, emphasis mine). *That's* the truth. *Those* are the words to cling to. Today and every day.

Jesus, You tell me that I have been given a sound mind. Somewhere along the way, I feel like I lost it. I forget that I'm fighting a spiritual battle and that those battles often start in the mind. Help me fight. Help me navigate these mind games and recognize them as lies. I can't do that without You. Teach me to rely on Your strength and not my own. In my attempt to control myself, I often forget to hand over the reins. Remind me. May I hear Your voice above the deafening sound of my Goliath's voice. Amen.

CHALLENGE

Meditate on 2 Timothy 1:7 (KJV). Memorize it. Stick it on your fridge. Write it down. Share it with someone. Speak it—not in your head. Out loud. When you're tempted to worry, speak it. When anxiety sucks the air from your lungs, speak it. When sleep is hard to find, speak it. When thoughts overwhelm, speak it. Tell Satan to get behind you—he has no place in the presence of Jesus Christ, who is *in* you. Be as relentless as your worry.

14

NAME

Israel and the Philistines were drawing up their lines facing each other. David left his things with the keeper of supplies, ran to the battle lines and greeted his brothers. As he was talking with them, Goliath, the Philistine champion from Gath, stepped out from his lines and shouted his usual defiance, and David heard it. When the Israelites saw the man, they all ran from him in great fear. . . . David asked the men standing near him, "Who is this uncircumcised Philistine that he should defy the armies of the living God?"
—1 Samuel 17:21–24, 26

For forty days and forty nights, Goliath rose in defiance against the Israelite army. During that time, David, the youngest of eight, tended his father's sheep. His three older brothers followed Saul into war. (Which, as we've read, didn't seem to be going very well.) David's father, Jesse, not having heard from his sons in weeks, asked David to go to the battlegrounds with bread and cheese to find out what was going on. He wanted assurance of their well-being (1 Sam. 17:12–19).

David, an early riser, took care of his first responsibility: the sheep.

He ensured the flock was well cared for by a fellow shepherd, and then set out for the Valley of Elah in obedience. When he arrived, the armies appeared to be at a critical juncture. The men were securing their positions, shouting the battle cry, and preparing to face the Philistine army again. Seeing the flurry of activity, David handed the bread and cheese to the keeper of supplies and raced onto the field to greet his brothers (1 Sam. 17:20–22).

We're not told what was said, but we do witness a rude interruption. Goliath, his ego fully bloated and busting at the seams, stepped forward and shouted his usual defiance. It wasn't anything new. It was the same routine. His material was old—words on repeat— and yet, his repetition continued to pay off. The Israelites, though flanked in armor and prepared for battle, fled in shame—again. This had already happened for forty days and forty nights. Do the math. That's eighty times they likely geared up for battle and then gave up before it even began.

But take note of an important distinction: David *heard.* The Israelites *saw.*

Forty days ago, the Israelites heard Goliath's defiance and fled (1 Sam. 17:11). *Now, they just had to see him coming.*

When our Goliath takes his stand day after day, we have a choice: dwell on the anxious thoughts or take them captive. Warranted or not, an anxious thought can quickly morph into worry when we don't pounce on it quickly.

Remember: how you feel isn't wrong. An anxious thought isn't sinful. However, cuddling up with anxious thoughts and holding them close ultimately feeds your giant's ego, which pulls your trust away from God and thrusts it onto earthly things. *That's* sinful. *That's* worry.

Keep in mind that an anxiety disorder is part disease (a biological imbalance) and part addiction (a choice). Therefore, you *can* choose to take captive that thought—that bellowed defiance from across the valley—and cling to truth, putting your trust in God. If it weren't so, God wouldn't have called us to that practice or called us not to worry (see 2 Cor. 10:5 and Matt. 6:25–34).

The other option is to allow that thought to rent space in your mind. Give it room to grow and develop into several thoughts until it mutates into worry. When we choose the latter, Goliath is no longer a giant on the other side of the ring; he's a monster that can't be ignored. What began as a whispered remark at the start of the day transforms into an angry, self-deprecating beast. And he'll continue to taunt you and tempt you to believe his pretty little lies. Likely, he laces his lies with some truth, twisting the truth just slightly so it's still believable. After all, your worries don't seem *entirely* unprecedented, right?

If he can't have your soul, he'll do everything in his power to make you as ineffective for Christ as possible.

Our enemy will contort the words of God, crafting them so precisely so they are believed. He did the same thing to Eve in the garden (see Gen. 3:1–7). How quickly we forget that a truth sprinkled with even an ounce of untruth is a lie. Don't you see? This isn't new material. Satan has used the same strategy since the very beginning of time. It's a weapon of mass destruction, and it does the job well. If he can't have your soul, he'll do everything in his power to make you as ineffective for Christ as possible.

And there's no better way to do that than by gaining a foothold in your mind.

David is a new set of eyes and ears on the battlefield. He hadn't heard Goliath's taunts until now. He hadn't been poisoned by the verbal attacks. He was hearing this for the very first time—and he was offended.

David saw clearly and therefore could speak clearly to the army. He saw Goliath for who he was and wasn't about to give him the luxury of taking another stand.

How could David see clearly when Saul and his army couldn't break free from the shackles of fear? There was one very big distinction: the Spirit of God had left Saul (1 Sam. 16:14) because he continued to be disobedient. But God was with David (1 Sam. 16:18). David saw with God's eyes. David abided in God's Word, meditating on it as he tended to the sheep.

Abiding in Christ, relying on His strength, and remaining in His Word makes an enormous difference.

David called Goliath an "uncircumcised Philistine." Those words, heavy with contempt, were said to remind the Israelite army, and his brothers in particular, of who stood before them. This giant was not in a covenant relationship with God. He was not under the promise and provision of the Lord.[1] He challenged the army of the *living* God, and for David that was unbearable. It sent righteous indignation coursing through his body. *How could they forget the promises of God?* He likely wondered. *How could they cower beneath this uncircumcised Philistine in fear? He defies God!*

It is important to name your Goliath as David did. To identify him. You may not be up against an uncircumcised Philistine, but you are up against something. Call him by name. In doing so, you ultimately size him up to the strength, power, and majesty of God.

Sometimes it takes a fresh set of eyes to name your Goliath. It can take someone on the outside looking in to see your giant for who he really is. Perhaps a counselor, friend, or family member. It's so easy to believe, *This is just who I am. It's how I think. It'll never go away. I'm a worrier. I must have been born this way. I'm just a perfection-ist. Freedom, recovery . . . it isn't possible.*

Every time you let his lies linger, you choose bondage.

That is what our enemy would like you to believe. He'd like to keep you prisoner within your own mind, enslaved to your thoughts. He'd like worry to steal your joy and rob you of sleep. He'd like to keep you from stepping out in faith, from taking risks, from rejecting your fears. Every time you let his lies linger, you choose bondage.

Rather than define *yourself* by your giant's words, define *him*. Name *him*.

Worry: irrational fear that prevents me from becoming all that God wants me to be and causes me to be stagnant in my walk with Christ.

Fear: chains that keep me in bondage to my paralyzing angst and keep me from enjoying life in abundance and freedom.

Panic: an uncontrollable emotion that is *not* of God—a terrifying experience that the enemy enjoys watching me suffer from.

Your giant may be named Worry, Fear, or Panic, but there's an even bigger, stealthier enemy that stands behind him, directing his every move. And who is he?

He's a liar.
He's a thief.

He's a murderer (see John 8:44, 10:10).

His name is Satan, and he has no place in the presence of Jesus Christ, who resides within you!

Satan has robbed you of peace, joy, and freedom for far too long. When you call your giant by name, when you define him and place the enemy's taunts before the intense power of Christ, it can make your blood boil. When you recognize how he's defied your right to freedom as a child of God, it's maddening. You are a child of the King. Your giant is nothing but an uncircumcised Philistine who is *not* under the promise or provision of Jesus Christ. But *you* are.

Lord, help me define my enemy. Not as I have in the past, but as you have in Scripture. I need to be reminded of his deceitful motives. Open my eyes as I study Satan so that I have all the ammunition I need to fight him on the battlefield. Help me remember who You are and who I am through You. Help me lean into Your strength, not my own. And once again, help me to surrender moment to moment. Amen.

CHALLENGE

Make a list with two columns. In one column, define Satan as he's defined in Scripture. Spend time meditating on this. Describe him. Then, in the other column, describe your God, your Savior. Pin that list to your wall. Keep it handy because you'll need reminders at times. And you'll need it on the battlefield.

15

LABELS

*David said to Saul, "Let no one lose heart on account of this
Philistine; your servant will go and fight him."
Saul replied, "You are not able to go out against this Philistine
and fight him; you are only a boy, and he has been a fighting man
from his youth."*
—1 Samuel 17:32–33

When I decided to step onto the battlefield, having strongly
resolved to put my Goliath in the ground, I knew it would take tremendous sacrifice and strength. I knew life would bear down firm
and press even harder before releasing me slowly. I anticipated getting filthy as I crawled through the trenches of my past in an effort
to shake off its shackles. I knew life was going to change—that
things were going to get messy. But I didn't expect soft, consoling
voices to encourage me to lower my expectations.

"You have an anxiety disorder," I was told. "You'll learn to manage it."

"Worry isn't a sin," a well-meaning friend said. "God would just
prefer us not to worry."

If there was no freedom from worry, why fight hard just to win a mediocre, managed state of mind? Freedom had to be a possibility—otherwise, there was no hope.

And what was freedom? Perhaps it wasn't the absence of the giant, but the freedom to stand over its lies, demands, and ruthless attacks. My giant could reside in the realms of Gath, but not on *my* territory. Freedom was no longer obeying the "authority" of worry's taunts and whispered fears. Freedom was living out from underneath its heavy hand and residing, instead, under the mighty hand of Christ.

When I fell so far that I could fall no further, God told me to fight. He challenged me: *what are you willing to sacrifice to find freedom?*

After tremendous prayer and counsel, I quit my job, leaving behind a career I thought I would never return to. It was the end of an era. A good run. I felt as though I was failing by walking away, but I knew I couldn't continue in the state I was in.

It was the hardest thing I'd ever done.

I sacrificed my pride and checked into counseling. I had been down that road a thousand times, but *this* time, *I* chose it. Not for anyone else, but for myself.

I went on medication and stayed under the watchful eye of a doctor. I cannot stress enough that part of an anxiety disorder is biological and chemical in nature. You may need medication for a season. Don't believe the lie that you need a pill because you don't have enough faith. I used to believe that—and it couldn't be further from the truth.

When I left my job, I could no longer physically function. I was absolutely crippled: paralyzed. I distinctly remember telling my husband several times: I cannot live this way. I *will not* live this way. It felt like a slow death.

I was desperate—at the end of a fraying, tattered rope.

So when I was quietly told that I would learn to *manage* my anxiety disorder, my hope cracked. Manage? Management means being on call, in control, in charge. No, one day I would learn how to let *God* manage my anxiety. After all, managing my anxiety is how I found myself in this dark place.

Yes, I tend to give my anxious thoughts room to breathe. I'm more wound up than most. But I do not believe I have to *live* in a state of panic or worry. I do not believe I have to *live* crippled. I can break the cycle of anxiety for my children by allowing God to break the cycle of anxiety within me. I believe there is freedom in Christ. Total freedom, total rest. If there wasn't, He wouldn't have said there was (see Gal. 5:1; John 8:36; 2 Cor. 3:17; and Matt. 11:28 for examples).

> **No, one day I would learn how to let *God* manage my anxiety. After all, managing my anxiety is how I found myself in this dark place.**

Just as a binge eater has to stay more aware of her choices walking through the buffet line, I have to work harder at taking my thoughts captive.

Saul took one look at David and said that he was too young to fight. "You are not able," Saul said. It wasn't an opinion. It was a declaration over the young boy: a label.

The wayward king looked David up and down, noting his stature, age, and experience, and failed to take into account the power of God. Yes, he was young. Yes, he was inexperienced. Yes, I'm a perfectionist. Yes, I have a tendency toward anxiousness. However,

Saul—and the well-meaning people around you—saw only the flesh standing before him. David was young. He had no military training. He was a shepherd boy—surely no match for the greatest of the Philistine army.

But David didn't miss a beat:

> Your servant has been keeping his father's sheep. When a lion or a bear came and carried off a sheep from the flock, I went after it, struck it and rescued the sheep from its mouth. When it turned on me, I seized it by its hair, struck it and killed it. Your servant has killed both the lion and the bear; this uncircumcised Philistine will be like one of them, because he has defied the armies of the living God. The LORD who delivered me from the paw of the lion and the paw of the bear will deliver me from the hand of this Philistine. (1 Sam. 17:34–37)

David didn't put up a defense for his age. He didn't try to convince Saul that he was capable as a result of practiced military training. Rather, David did what so many of us forget to do: he recounted the past and gave glory to the One who brought him through each prior trial. He answered fear with faith.

We often forget what God has already delivered us from. Surely, Goliath was a greater threat than the lion or the bear, but in David's wisdom, he knew that if God could deliver him from the beasts of the field, He could deliver him from the threat of mankind.

David relied not on his own strength, but the Lord's. He was not going into battle alone.

And neither are you.

When you choose to fight your Goliath, you may be encouraged by others to lower your expectations of healing. You may receive a quizzical look when you take that leap of faith, praying that freedom will catch you whole. You'll be labeled "disordered" by many. Others will think you're taking the fight a bit too seriously—after all, it's *only* worry.

But remember Who stands behind you. Remember Who's fighting on your behalf. Remember what the Lord *calls* you—not what man *labels* you. Choose to stand behind His shield, His protection. Lean into His strength and recount the past. Choose to recall all the ways He has delivered you, saved you, consoled you, and freed you.

No matter how big your Goliath is, He's no match for our God.

Father, remind me of Your grace and Your deliverance. Bring to my mind all the circumstances You've carried me through in the past. When well-meaning people

> **Remember what the Lord *calls* you—not what man *labels* you.**

encourage me to take things slow and steady, to lower my expectations for freedom, help me remember what You've said. What You call me. You call me Your child. You call me Yours. Amen.

CHALLENGE

You are a perfectionist. That statement could absolutely be true about you. You may worry a lot. Also true. David was young. Truth. David wasn't a skilled army brute. Truth. But David was *able*, and so are you. You are able to fight, not in your own strength, but in Christ's strength. Take some time to recall all the ways God has provided for you in the past, all the ways He has delivered you. Write them down in your journal. The same God who delivered you then will deliver you now.

16

WEAPONS

*Then Saul dressed David in his own tunic. He put a coat of armor
on him and a bronze helmet on his head. David fastened on his
sword over the tunic and tried walking around, because he was
not used to them.*
*"I cannot go in these," he said to Saul, "because I am not used
to them." So he took them off. Then he took his staff in his hand,
chose five smooth stones from the stream, put them in the pouch
of his shepherd's bag and, with his sling in his hand, approached
the Philistine.*
—1 Samuel 17:38–40

For nearly six weeks, Goliath's challenge had been met with silence.
Even Saul's reward—his daughter's hand in marriage, tremendous
wealth, and tax-free living—was not enough to entice a single soldier onto the battlefield (see 1 Sam. 17:25). Much was at stake: lives,
freedom, security—the winner would take all. But for forty days,
the Israelite army stood frozen, unwilling to send one of their own
into combat. Until now.

David steps onto the scene, exuding a confidence unlike anything Saul had seen in weeks. He was so sure, so strong in faith. A

faith Saul had lost (see 1 Sam. 16:14). Although David was young, untrained, unqualified, and unfit for the job, Saul had little choice. He was desperate. So desperate, he ultimately decided to leave the fate of the entire kingdom in the hands a mere shepherd boy.

"Go, and the LORD be with you," Saul responded (v. 37). Perhaps he hung his head in despair. Or maybe he was intrigued by the boy's unwavering confidence—even trusted it. Either way, Saul had no other choice. If he didn't let David fight, they would be on their side of the hill for an unforeseen number of days.

So, being a seasoned veteran, Saul dressed David in his own armor. But as one can imagine, it was clunky. Heavy. Unfamiliar. The helmet likely tipped forward, shielding the boy's eyes. The brass tunic too cumbersome and restricting. David was not used to such attire, and so he removed it all, going forth entirely unarmed.

But was he *really* unarmed?

Hardly.

David spent tremendous time in the fields with his sheep, and while he sat on the hillside, he meditated on the law and wrote beautiful songs to the Lord. Though he only had a few rudimentary weapons slung over his shoulders, he was covered in the armor of God, a spiritual armor. For this was more than just a battle of brute force, it was a spiritual battle—one in which God would be glorified.

So David did as David knew. He took his staff and chose five smooth stones from the river's edge. He placed them in his shepherd's bag and, with sling in hand, stepped across the battle line.

These were weapons that David had grown accustomed to: weapons he likely used to fight off the beasts that threatened to harm his flock. His bare arms and legs and lack of protection would further prove to the Philistine army that the battle was God's, and that the victory was not by David's own strength. Surely, it would take a miracle to overcome such a beast of a man without the proper gear.

But David rested in the unseen armor of the Lord. He was not alone. He was fully equipped in the eyes of the Lord and therefore was the perfect vessel for reclaiming the Israelites' rightful place.

David was wise and went into battle prepared. He took five stones and slipped them into his shepherd's bag. In his hand, he carried his slingshot—not the forked slingshot we know today. It was formed using two strips of leather, and a wide panel in the middle held the stone.[1] It could be lethal, but it was considered low-budget artillery compared to the Philistine's state-of-the-art iron weaponry (see Judg. 20:16).

But this didn't sway David's confidence. His confidence rested in the extraordinary might and power of God—not in the equipment he carried.

As we fight worry, we may be intimidated by how large our giant appears. We fear we don't have the weapons to fight or the skill to compete. But that's just it—we *don't.*

David was not equipped to battle Goliath. Neither are we equipped to battle worry. Not alone, anyway. Don't you see? *The victory was even sweeter because David was destined to fail in the eyes of man.* The coming victory would further emphasize God's incredible power and majesty because it could not have been possible without divine intervention.

We must put our trust in God. We must clothe ourselves in the spiritual armor described in Ephesians 6:14–17. Then, and only then, do we stand a chance against our Goliath.

Lord, I often rely on my own strength to fight. But it has failed me time and time again. I know I must find my confidence in Your strength, and Your strength alone. As I wage war against this Goliath in my life, I ask that you furnish me with spiritual armor. May my confidence come from You. And may You, Father, get ALL the glory. Amen.

CHALLENGE

Ephesians 6:10–13 says:

> Finally, be strong in the Lord and in his mighty power. Put on the full armor of God so that you can take your stand against the devil's schemes. For our struggle is not against flesh and blood, but against the rulers, against the authorities, against the powers of this dark world and against the spiritual forces of evil in the heavenly realms. Therefore, put on the full armor of God, so that when the day of evil comes, you may be able to stand your ground, and after you have done everything, to stand.

Our battle is against the enemy. Tempting us to worry is just one of his many schemes. Meditate on these verses. Recognize your battle as a spiritual one. And put on the spiritual armor necessary to fight. Move forward with the belt of truth buckled around your waist, the breastplate of righteousness in place, your feet fitted with the readiness that comes from the gospel of peace, the shield of faith, the helmet of salvation, and the sword of the Spirit (paraphrased; see Eph. 6:14–17). Then, when worry takes its stand each morning and evening, you'll be able to stand your ground—and win.

17

WORDS

Meanwhile, the Philistine, with his shield bearer in front of him, kept coming closer to David. He looked David over and saw that he was only a boy, ruddy and handsome, and he despised him. He said to David, "Am I a dog, that you come at me with sticks?" And the Philistine cursed David by his gods. "Come here," he said, "and I'll give your flesh to the birds of the air and the beasts of the field!" David said to the Philistine, "You come against me with sword and spear and javelin, but I come against you in the name of the Lord *Almighty, the God of the armies of Israel, whom you have defied. This day the* Lord *will hand you over to me, and I'll strike you down and cut off your head. Today I will give the carcasses of the Philistine army to the birds of the air and the beasts of the earth, and the whole world will know that there is a God in Israel. All those gathered here will know that it is not by sword or spear that the* Lord *saves; for the battle is the* Lord's*, and he will give all of you into our hands."*
—1 Samuel 17:41–47

Breaths came broken and tight. Trembling fingers clenched the wheel, wrists grinding my dry skin back and forth over the hard plastic. Nausea rose up, inching precariously close to the back of my throat. I blinked back tears, hard.

You've made a terrible mistake

You're not ready for this.

You're destined to fail.

The words, like heavy hands, dipped my hope slowly beneath the surface of the water. It was as if my throat was held tight by a firm grasp, relentless. The muscles in my back, neck, and shoulders screamed for mercy, tight with ache and strain.

It had only been a day or two.

And yet, as I drove to the building on the hill where my chance at a career on my own terms sat, anxiety hooked me from behind.

God had given me a gift, a love of words, an eye for detail. Yet, Satan had used that gift against me . . .

You'll let them down and have no one to blame but yourself.

If you can't perform perfectly, you might as well forfeit entirely.

I couldn't drive fast enough to outrun my thoughts. They haunted me, chased me. Three months had passed. Three solid months of recovery, therapy, and rest, only to be caught up in a fury of doubt. Only to be left flailing for stability of thought. God had given me a gift, a love of words, an eye for detail. Yet, Satan had used that gift against me, filling my mind with panic over misplaced hyphens, unnecessary commas, and grammatical inconsistencies.

When others had nightmares about death and monsters, my nightmares were riddled with misspelled words plastered over catalog covers and billboards.

No, no, no, I thought, the double yellow lines whipping past me on the highway. *No, please, not now.* Tears stung my eyes and threatened to spill down my cheeks.

I had been fighting for so long, and now this? How did he sneak in? Panic crept up my spine, my heart beating faster and faster with each second. I turned on the air conditioning.

Finally, it struck me, the words my mother encouraged me to speak out loud.

"Get behind me, Satan," I whimpered from a wounded place in my heart. The words came weak, trembling. "Get behind me, Satan," I repeated, this time with a bit more energy.

"You have no place in my mind, in my heart, or before Jesus Christ who lives in me," I screamed, broken, at the windshield. I squeezed the wheel tighter. "I have been given a sound mind. Get behind me, Satan! You have no authority in my life."

As the words came, they came louder, stronger, firmer. With each repetition, the fury in my heart grew. Suddenly, the monster I was driving toward seemed a bit less threatening, a bit smaller than he did just a moment ago. And as he shrunk in size, the boldness in my heart—once nothing more than a smoldering ember at best—began to burn a bit brighter.

The remainder of my commute was spent bellowing God's promises out loud. I spoke them as if Satan himself sat in the passenger seat. He had no authority in my life. He had no place in my thoughts. Worry, his weapon of choice, was being evicted. No longer allowed to rent space in my mind; not today anyway, not now.

As I pulled into the parking lot and came to an abrupt halt, I let out an exasperated sigh. I was mentally exhausted from the fight, yet emotionally charged and empowered. I sat in the car for just a minute longer and prayed a quick prayer over the day. And then I grabbed my piping hot coffee and my purse, stuffed with chamomile tea, a journal, and my devotional, and walked toward the glass doors of the building. Chin held high, steady strides.

And I continued to remind the enemy where his place was. When Goliath saw David crossing the valley, he must have rolled his eyes, pointed, and let out a boisterous laugh. David was the ant and Goliath the shoe. David didn't stand a chance.

And Goliath mocked him.

"Am I a dog, that you come at me with sticks?" he chided. "Come here, and I'll give your flesh to the birds of the air and the beasts of the field!" (v. 43–44).

Just as my giant tried to convince me to turn back, to run, Goliath mocked David's courage. Worry is abrasive, crude, and can be exceptionally mean, reminding you of every weakness, every "what if." David's giant was no different.

But David stood his ground. Because he put on the full armor of God before crossing the battle line, he had the strength to stand.

And he fought Goliath with truth.

You come against me with sword and spear and javelin, but I come against you in the name of the LORD Almighty, the God of the armies of Israel, whom you have defined. This day the LORD will hand you over to me, and I'll strike you down and cut off your head. Today I will give the carcasses of the Philistine army to the birds of the air and the beasts of the earth, and the whole world will know that there is a God in Israel. All those gathered here will know that it is not by sword or spear that the LORD saves; for the battle is the LORD's, and he will give all of you into our hands. (v. 45-47)

Wow. David didn't mess around. He spoke with such power, such might, such courage. I aspire to be like this young shepherd boy, so full of confidence in the God he serves.

When worry stares us in the face, mocks our efforts, and attempts to strangle our hope, we must speak—out loud—against the thoughts that exist internally. This is a spiritual battle. A heart battle.

He knows he cannot have your soul, so he will do everything in his power to ill equip you for the plan God has for you.

When the enemy taunts and sneers and the stench of his venomous words cause your hope to grow faint, fight him with words. Not with your words—with God's words. Worry is just a battle tactic Satan uses in the fight for your heart. He knows he cannot have your soul, so he will do everything in his power to ill equip you for the plan God has for you. He'll tempt your mind with lies so that the truth becomes a fog.

Don't let him forget his place in the presence of the Almighty, *living* God. Remind him who is Lord of your life. Crush him beneath the power of Christ's promises. And stand. Stand firm. Stand ready. And be vigilant with your tongue.

Jesus, I live in a state of fear. I cower at my giant's taunts and lies. I can hardly stand physically beneath his words, let alone spiritually. Help me to clothe myself in Your armor. Help me resist the lies by speaking the truth out loud. I know Satan has no authority in my life, but over time, he's convinced me oth-

erwise. **Help me put him in his place. Help me fight against worry and bring glory to Your name. May I speak Your truths and promises with divine confidence so that I can live the life You've designed for me. Amen.**

CHALLENGE

Speak the truth out loud. When an anxious thought is born, takes refuge in your heart, and grows up into worry, speak truth against it. Remember, this is not just a physical battle. This is a spiritual battle. When you're in your cubical, whisper the truth out loud. When you're with friends, escape to the bathroom and speak the words aloud into the mirror. In the grocery store or a public place, mutter the words softly. Practice speaking truth. The more you speak it, the more you'll believe it. And the greater a threat you'll become.

18

CHARGE

As the Philistine moved closer to attack him, David ran quickly
toward the battle line to meet him.
—1 Samuel 17:48

My body woke. But before my eyelids released, I felt it. Bearing down. I opened my eyes and stared tiredly at the wall beside our bed. I had awoken in the wee hours of the morning, and the songbirds were just beginning their sweet melody, growing louder by the minute. Then the obnoxious cries began—the piercing sounds of the crow and blue jay, and other unfortunate noises. I rolled over. My husband slept so soundly, so peacefully. I swung my legs over the edge of the bed and stood to remove the window fan, quietly shutting the window and drawing the blinds.

The sounds remained, though muffled. And then my thoughts began to mingle with them. And suddenly, a panic swelled in my chest. Anxiety, like a strong tide, pulled me into its clutches, drawing me close.

I lay back down and rolled over. Repositioned. Squeezed my eyelids tight. The way they were before. They way they were supposed to have stayed.

But it didn't keep the thoughts out. They whirled around like tumultuous ocean waves, growing greater and stronger as they closed in on the sandy surface.

I tossed and turned, trying to rid my mind of the thoughts. As if enough tossing and turning and jostling would make them fall out of my brain.

When that didn't work, I tried to will them away, too tired to do much else. I took refuge beneath the cool sheets and the plume of our down comforter. Maybe they wouldn't find me there. At least not until the alarm sounded. And then, pure exhaustion took over my body, and I slipped quietly into a numbing sleep.

David responded quite differently as Goliath neared the battle line and peered at him from the other side. As the beast stepped forward, David took off toward him, arms and legs pumping hard and fast as he raced across the valley to meet him.

The giant made the first defiant move, but David immediately gained the upper hand and remained several strides ahead for the remainder of the battle.

I sought comfort in sleep. In retreat. In cowering. In pushing them away, rather than pulling them closer for the slaughter.

I couldn't help but think, *What if I had turned to face my thoughts, charging toward them with fury?*

Instead, I sought comfort in sleep. In retreat. In cowering. In pushing them away, rather than pulling them closer for the slaughter.

David showed no fear because his trust was in the living God, not in his sheer strength or might. How often do we forget this in the midst of our fight?

We must make the first move. Perhaps if we ran toward our anxiety with the supernatural power and strength of God Almighty beneath our feet, we would become a tangible threat. Our giants may creep close again. But maybe they'd come forward a bit more reluctantly, fearing our hostility and the supernatural strength within us.

As children of God, we must rush the enemy. We must make the first move. We must gain the upper hand. Take the first step and sprint. Show the enemy that he has no power over our actions or over our minds because we were bought by the blood of Jesus, and it is through His power, His might, and His strength that we overcome.

Because let's face it: with God on our side, we are a greater threat than our Goliath could ever hope to be.

Jesus, spur me on. Urge me forward. May I make the first move with bold confidence toward my Goliath. Give me a hunger in my soul to run out, as David did, to meet him. To stand toe-to-toe with him so that You get all the glory. Help me remain confident that we will win because You go before me and the battle is Yours. The enemy already knows that, and I know he doesn't want me to catch on. Help me fight. Help me fight hard. And help me gird up the energy to *run* toward that poisonous beast. Amen.

CHALLENGE

The next time worry tries to take you from behind, turn to face it. Make the first move. Don't let it keep the upper hand. Speak the truth aloud, collapse to your knees in silent prayer—know which tactics you'll use to bring it down. Plan ahead and then rush the enemy with all you've got.

19

FAITH

Reaching into his bag and taking out a stone, he slung it and struck the Philistine on the forehead. The stone sank into his forehead, and he fell facedown on the ground.
So David triumphed over the Philistine with a sling and a stone; without a sword in his hand he struck down the Philistine and killed him.
David ran and stood over him. He took hold of the Philistine's sword and drew it from the scabbard. After he killed him, he cut off his head with the sword.
When the Philistines saw that their hero was dead, they turned and ran.
—1 Samuel 17:49–51

Running towards your giant without a strategy or battle plan is like jumping into a pool without knowing how to swim. It could result in catastrophe.

David may not have had military training or skill, but he used his own familiar, time-tested method of defense. There were famous slingers in Israel—so skilled that they could sling a stone at a hair and not miss (see Judg. 20:16). Goliath knew this, but he was proud, cocky (not to mention unpleasant), and it wouldn't be far-fetched to suggest that he came forward with the beaver of his helmet open, leaving his forehead exposed.[1]

As David ran onto the battlefield, he reached into his shepherd's bag and searched for one of the five smooth, baseball-sized stones he had gathered from the brook moments ago.[2]

But why did David choose five stones? Was it because he feared missing? I doubt it. After all, the speech he just gave likely dropped the jaws of his own comrades. And he *ran* out to meet his adversary. Had he been afraid of missing, he would have hung back a bit and waited for a more opportune moment. He'd sneak up on him. Attack at night.

Perhaps, as some suggest, David knew His God could get the job done with one stone, but chose four more should he encounter Goliath's relatives (see 2 Sam. 21:20–22).[3]

But he also knew that he'd be required to play his part in the fight. So he rushed the giant—immediately going on the offensive. Not the defensive.

David ran to the battlefield *prepared*. His heart and soul were filled with the promise of God, and his shepherd's sack was filled with choice weapons—tools familiar to him and proven to be previously effective.

We must approach our giant with a similar battle strategy: we must cover ourselves in the courage and strength of God and disassemble our giant with a selection of God-given tools. Your toolbox looks different than mine because we must use tools and strategies that are familiar to us personally. David knew the battle was the Lord's, but he also knew that he'd be required to play his part in the fight. So he rushed the giant—immediately going on the offensive. Not the defensive.

David didn't panic. He didn't wait for Goliath. He accepted the challenge and reached into his bag, pulled out a stone, and placed it into his sling. He twirled it around his head in circles and then released it, sending it careening through the air at lightning speed. This wasn't just a rock; it was a powerful force, a lethal weapon, whipping through the air at what could have been one hundred yards per second.[4] That's nearly two hundred miles per hour.

And then the stone met its target.

It struck the enemy hard, sinking deep into the giant's forehead, as the Philistine army looked on in horror as their prized hero's knees buckled, sending him crumbling to the ground.

With Christ's power and supernatural strength, you can stand against your giant. You can watch your giant weaken at the knees.

David didn't raise his hands in celebration just yet. He ran to the fallen soldier and stood over him. A young boy standing over the carcass of a monster. The picture of triumph. Just like you'll one day stand over your worry in victory. Though the giant was already dead, David erased any lingering skepticism among the armies and drew the Philistine's heavy sword from the scabbard and beheaded him. *Let there be no doubt*, he must have been thinking, taking the giant's head as a token of victory.

Can you hear the thunderous roar of the Israelites as David held Goliath's head in his hands, proof of defeat? Do you see the army lift their swords and shields in a triumphant cheer? I do. I feel the shake of the earth as their cheers echoed across the valley and reverberated against the hills on either side. And in the picture I paint in my own mind, I see David looking toward the heavens—a subtle tribute to the real Hero that day.

With Christ's power and supernatural strength, you can stand against your giant. You can watch your giant weaken at the knees. But you have to be brazen, brutish, and bold in your approach.

You must follow David's steps. Track his footprints. Learn from him. Learn from his story.

It took David just one heroic swing to bring the Philistine down. It may take you more than one swing, more than one rock. Worry is a beast that can require a lifetime on the battlefield. The longer and harder you fight, the more worn and defenseless the giant becomes. You may have to fight long and hard, but I can tell you this: it won't *conquer* you. It may gain an upper hand or leave you battered and bruised at times. But it won't win. Not when you fight on behalf of the *living* God.

With His power behind you, your giant won't have the strength to stand.

Heavenly Father, help me rush my giant. Remind me that I must face You in order to face him. It can be so easy to forget. Fill my sling with the stones required to slay this beast, this monster rising up and overshadowing every part of my day. The enemy is cocky. He's a stalker. He watches my every move. Sees where I'm weak. And then he meets me in those weak places—far more prepared at defeating me than I am at defeating him. Help me identify the tools You've given me to slay him. May You get all the glory when my giant tumbles to the ground. Amen.

CHALLENGE

You must allow God to work through you. You must stand in obedience as David did and be willing to do whatever God calls you to do (see Acts 13:22). You must move under divine direction. I find that when I am living in obedience, my anxiety isn't as aggressive. When I write, as God has called me to, the swells of panic come less frequently. Obedience is never easy. It means work. It means rushing onto the battlefield when the odds are against you. But obedience is what set David apart from the rest of the Israelites. He submitted to the authority of God. He heeded divine direction—even when it seemed unnatural. And as a result, God used him in a mighty and awesome way. What has God been calling you to that you've been reluctant in pursuing? Delayed obedience is disobedience. Had David delayed in rushing the giant, what would have happened? We'll never know this side of heaven.

Take inventory of your heart today. Is there an area of your life you haven't submitted to God? Sit in the quiet, in the still, and reflect. And choose today to live obediently, regardless of what you think it might cost you. And remember: the same Power that defeated Goliath through David is the Power that will ultimately crush your Goliath.

20

DAVID

*Then the men of Israel and Judah surged forward with a shout
and pursued the Philistines to the entrance of Gath and to the
gates of Ekron. Their dead were strewn along the Shaaraim road
to Gath and Ekron.*
—1 Samuel 17:52

The battle was over. Victory was theirs. The Philistine army, stunned by their sudden loss, fell back, while the men of Israel and Judah trailed behind them in hot pursuit. Perhaps David led the charge. Surging forward, he led the men on a stampede of epic proportions, chasing the enemy all the way to Gath—the birthplace of Goliath—and even further to the gates of Ekron, about ten miles northwest of the valley.[1]

> **Abandoned camps on either side of the valley sat lifeless, the ground left alone to absorb the blood of the Philistines' finest warrior.**

Back to where they belonged.

Meanwhile, the Valley of Elah grew quiet. Abandoned camps on either side of the valley sat lifeless, the ground left alone to absorb the blood of the Philistines' finest warrior.

When the Israelites returned to plunder the enemy's camp, David took Goliath's head to Jerusalem and put the Philistine's weapons in his own tent (see 1 Sam. 17:53–54). These symbols of victory—like trophies—acted, perhaps, as a pointed reminder to the Israelite army of what God was a capable of doing through man.

And even through a boy . . .

While we've come to the end of Goliath's story, David's story is just beginning. It's the beginning of a grand legacy, a rich heritage.

But why did God choose David as the one to take down Goliath? What made this shepherd boy stand out from among the soldiers?

I believe the answer is simple: *he abided in the Lord.*

Though David was young, he was already so familiar with the heartbeat of his Lord. And is it any wonder?

David spent countless hours watching and guarding his father's sheep. With the quiet of the fields around him, the gentle rattle of the sheep's cry, and countless hours beneath the hot sun, David likely spent significant time with the Lord.

He no doubt penned beautiful songs, much like prayers, from his place in the fields. Like the Psalms, some may have spilled from a lonely, abandoned soul. Others from fear or shame. But regardless of circumstance, David abided in God and the Lord was with him (see 1 Sam. 16:18, 17:37). He sought refuge, escape—every need— from the Lord, planting himself beside the constant flow of His wisdom, seeking it daily and often.

Jeremiah 17:7–8 says, "But blessed is the man who trusts in the LORD, whose confidence is in him. He will be like a tree planted by the water that sends out its roots by the stream. It does not fear when the heat comes; its leaves are always green. It has no worries in a year of drought and never fails to bear fruit."

As a tree planted beside a stream grows to great heights and its roots spread deep into the fertile earth, drawing up an abundance of nourishment, so does a person who plants him or herself in Christ. God's Word is like a stream, a gurgling, continuous flow of knowledge and wisdom. It's always moving, never stagnant, its current always pulling the reader closer and closer toward the heart of God.

The word "planted" in Hebrew can mean exactly that: planted. But it can also mean to be "transplanted."[2] We must uproot our trust in fear, the confidence we place in worry, and plant it in the faithfulness of Christ, by the stream that never dries up.

David did this. David put his trust, reliance, and confidence in God and found security in His embrace. Surely storms brewed and his confidence at times drained, but he remained planted because his roots had spread far and deep. When winds came, he remained sure. Secure. And so his roots continued to grow out and closer toward the stream, toward God's grace and provision.

Because David was rooted, because he planted his heart, trust, and faith in God long before Goliath rose up over the hillside, he did not fear when he heard the Philistine's mockery and belittling roar. He did not shrivel up at the sight of his monstrosity. No. His leaves were green; he was spiritually healthy. The word "green" not only evokes a sense of thriving and flourishing, it can mean "spreading."[3] David's spiritual health spread throughout the camp. Though the Israelites likely cringed as David approached the Philistine and shook their heads at his apparent foolishness, David went forth with unwavering faith. And he sent that giant tumbling to the ground. His courage and miraculous victory spurred the Israelite army ahead. And they chased the enemy, already retreating, out of their territory and then squandered their camp.

David's relationship with God was the only reason that Goliath fell facedown that day. David's complete trust and confidence in the Lord was the weapon that set him apart.

And Goliath couldn't stand.

We cannot fight on our own strength. We cannot thrive on our own diet of positive self-talk. We must drink in the Word of God, abide in His wisdom, trust in His leading, and remain fully confident in His plan for our future. We must encourage ourselves in the Lord, repeating His promises in our hearts and speaking them into our lives. Then, and only then, will our giants fall back.

Father, for so long—too long—my worry has been contagious, infecting everything around me. Teach me to abide in You so that I can spread something new: a spiritual health that will point others to You. I want to be a contagious disciple. Increase my faith so that others can see that my confidence rests in You and You alone. Amen.

CHALLENGE

We set dates and times for everything in our lives: meetings, doctor appointments, conference calls, and get-togethers. But do you set a date and time to meet with Jesus? Today, pick a time. If you're an early riser, commit to getting up fifteen minutes early. Night owl? Skip the sitcom and crack open your Bible. Set an alarm on your phone. Find an accountability partner. Do what it takes to make that a priority in your life. You must if you are to become like a tree planted by water. You will learn to live in freedom. Because when you abide, you thrive.

FRAGILE

freedom

FRAGILE

21

NEAR

The Lord is near. Do not be anxious about anything, but in everything, by prayer and petition, with thanksgiving, present your requests to God. And the peace of God, which transcends all understanding, will guard your hearts and your minds in Christ Jesus.
—Philippians 4:5–7

"Do not be anxious about anything," Paul writes.

To the anxious heart, that's like saying, "Don't scratch that itch." "Don't sneeze." "Don't blink."

An impossible request. An unattainable way of living.

To most, this verse reads hopeless. But take a closer look: Do not *be* anxious. *Be.* Paul is referring to a state of existence: the identity or condition of a person. He is imploring that the Philippians not *be* anxious. To dwell, to reside, to live in that state of mind. Paul is not saying that *feeling* anxious is wrong. For feelings are simply emotions that come and go like the tide. It's what we do with those emotions that matters.

> Feelings are simply emotions that come and go like the tide. It's what we do with those emotions that matter.

In this verse, the word "anxious" comes from the Greek word *merimnaō*, meaning "to worry, have anxiety, be concerned."[1] It's a verb. Remember: anxiety is a feeling; worry is a behavior.

We see the Greek word again in the well-known verses in Matthew 6:

> Therefore I tell you, do not **worry** about your life, what you will eat or drink; or about your body, what you will wear. Is not life more important than food, and the body more important than clothes? . . . Who of you by **worrying** can add a single hour to his life? And why do you **worry** about clothes? . . . So do not **worry**, saying, "What shall we eat?" or "What shall we drink?" or "What shall we wear?" For the pagans run after all these things, and your heavenly Father knows that you need them. But seek first his kingdom and his righteousness, and all these things will be given to you as well. Therefore do not **worry** about tomorrow, for tomorrow will **worry** about itself. Each day has enough trouble of its own. (v. 25, 27, 28, 31–34, emphasis mine)

Don't you see? It is not anxiety we must avoid. It's *worry*. The behavior. The choice. And it's just that: a choice. The words "worry" and "anxious" are often used interchangeably in modern-day speech and writing. But there's a stark difference. The Greek word used for "worry" in the verse above is the *same* Greek word used for "anxious" in Philippians.

Paul is imploring the Philippians, as Jesus did, not to be self-consumed with worry. Their focus was divided, as ours often is. We claim faith in Christ yet spend our time and energy worrying about work, school, our children, our spouses, our friends, finances—just about anything and everything outside our immediate control. We pull away our trust in Christ and place our faith in something entirely elusive: the unknown.

I heard my pastor once say that worry is not the *absence* of faith, but rather, worry is *misplaced* faith. Worry is evidence of faith—faith in oneself. In Matthew 6:30, Jesus even referred to those He was speaking to as having little faith because they were placing their concern in things that were counterproductive to the spread and influence of the gospel. Their worry divided their loyalty. It divided their trust. It put a question mark beside the provision of Jesus Christ.

So what is the antidote to that worry? Prayer and petition with thanksgiving (see Phil. 4:6). Each of which we've discussed in previous chapters. You can't be thankful and fearful

> **Worry is evidence of faith—faith in oneself.**

simultaneously, in the same way that darkness and light cannot coexist. When you pray with thanksgiving and place your anxious thoughts at the foot of the cross, you prevent worry from taking root in your heart and dividing your faith.

And we must pray, as Jesus did in the garden, with intensity, until the episode passes. And what is our reward? A peace that surpasses all understanding (see Phil. 4:7). A peace that overflows, one that can only come from the power of Jesus Christ. It washes away the anxiety and fear and replaces it with an inner tranquility so full it cannot be explained, only felt. And God, the same God who took out Goliath, will safeguard your heart and mind like an armed sentry, protecting you from perpetual insecurity.[2] And why does He say that He will guard our hearts? Because from the heart comes our thoughts (see Matt. 15:18–19). And from our thoughts come action. An anxious heart produces anxious thoughts, which

> **An anxious heart produces anxious thoughts, which produce worry. And worry robs us of joy.**

produce worry. And worry robs us of joy.

You'll find peace on your knees—for prayer is the ultimate form of surrender. It demonstrates your complete dependence on God. And peace—a beautiful, overwhelming peace—will saturate your soul in a way you've never experienced.

That is what freedom looks like. That's what freedom tastes like. That's what freedom feels like. Do you see it? Do you taste it? Do feel the soft caress of it over your soul? Maybe not yet. But as you toil daily, as you fight and pour your heart out to Jesus, He will fill the empty place in your mind, where your concern once harbored, with His everlasting peace. A peace beyond human comprehension, beyond what can be described with the written word. A transforming peace. And when you feel that peace for the first time, you'll begin to walk into freedom.

The Lord is near. He is so near, so close to the brokenhearted. And He longs to give you rest (see Ps. 34:18 and Matt. 11:28).

Lord, You say that You are near to the brokenhearted. That You will soak me in overwhelming peace if I give all my concerns to You with thanksgiving. I want to know that peace, Lord. Thank You for hearing me. Thank You for being near me. Thank You for Your Word and Your promises. Thank You for what You will accomplish through my weakness. I wait in anticipation for what You'll do. Amen.

CHALLENGE

A thankful heart is medicine for the soul. When we're wrought with worry and wrestling with anxiety, it's easy to get caught up in asking God for things: for peace, deliverance, freedom, provision, rescue. How often do we clothe those requests with thanksgiving? It's easy to forget, especially in the midst of panic. Practice thanksgiving. Meet the dawn with praise. Regardless of your situation, exude thanksgiving (see 1 Thess. 5:18). Honor Him in this way. I can promise you that this practice will reroute your attitude and bring hope to your circumstance, no matter how dire.

22

CHOOSE

Therefore, there is now no condemnation for those who are in Christ Jesus, because through Christ Jesus the law of the Spirit of life set me free from the law of sin and death.
—Romans 8:1–2

We each live by a belief system, a set of rules. It's how we both got to this place. There are standards and expectations—most of which are unattainable—that you hold yourself to, which more often than not produce negativity, self-condemnation, and low self-esteem. My rules are different than yours, which are different than the next person's. But regardless, they keep the wheel of anxiety churning.

Why do we have rules? I think it's to feel safe. To feel secure. To feel good. To feel valued. To feel worthy of something, anything. Rather than find security and rest in Christ, we seek to follow our well-intended rules to keep our minds at ease. When we break a rule, a trigger pulls, setting off a bout of anxiety or panic, which we feel we can't control—and often can't.

I unknowingly made up rules to help me feel secure: a calorie count to abide by; a number to maintain on the scale; rules about sauces and sweets and restaurants allowed. When I broke a rule, panic ensued, reaching into the very core of my being and working its way out through my pen. I'd call myself the worst names, inscribing them in my journal beside the column of numbers that didn't follow the guidelines I had drawn up. Words like a fortress around an inked tower of numerals that defined who I was.

The enemy used my mind as a weapon against me. And it nearly killed me.

Tomorrow was always a new day: a clean slate. A new tower of numbers that I vowed would add up *correctly.* That would follow the rules. Those rules, like guardrails, prevented me from tumbling into a ravine of regret. Like bumpered bowling lanes, I could go for gold without worrying about landing in the gutter. Without them? I felt anxious, like I had failed: failed God and failed myself.

I never lent myself any grace. Any leniency. No mercy. No forgiveness. And over time, I spiraled into a world that exists now only as a memory.

The enemy used my mind as a weapon against me. And it nearly killed me.

I found no truth in Romans 8:1–2. The enemy convinced me that I was an exception to the rule. That I had to prove myself worthy. That I deserved some sort of punishment. Surely condemnation would find me, even as a child of God. I believed the lie that I was not good enough, worthy enough, or even lovable. That God was pleased only by my performance. Those beliefs propelled me deeper into a battle with anxiety. Huddled on my bed, knees to my chest, and trembling in the dark. For years, that was me. So far from freedom. So entwined with worry. My giant had me by the throat.

But Romans 8:1–2 says there is no condemnation for those who are in Christ Jesus. None. You are not condemned for your belief system. You are not condemned for your mental tug-of-war. You are not condemned for your worry. You are not condemned for your fatigue or for the days you don't feel like fighting. There is *no* condemnation if you are a child of God. No matter what you are going through or how anxiety overtakes you, breaking you to your very core, it pales in comparison to what Jesus Christ accomplished on the cross. And it is because of that cross that you are free.

You are free to believe He can use you, or to believe you are useless. *Your choice will dictate your destiny.*

When you accepted Christ, your freedom was paid for, the debt erased. God declared you "not guilty" through the blood of His Son, Jesus Christ. But you must choose to accept that freedom.

Your greatest weakness, worry, is God's greatest opportunity. That's where He can shine the brightest.

But there's a choice: to believe you are condemned or to believe you are free. You are free to believe He can use you, or to believe you are useless. *Your choice will dictate your destiny.*

As a follower of Christ, you're already free, but you must choose to *live* in that freedom today. Jesus has already unlocked the prison gates. You can stay in your cell, living chained to your old life. Or you can live free by taking hold of the truths in Romans 8:1–2 and crawling out from underneath the heavy weight of condemnation. I once heard it said that choosing freedom doesn't just free you *from* something, it frees you *to be* something else. Free to be used. Free to be a testimony. Free to live victoriously, as Jesus intended. He did not die a brutal death and carry the weight of every sin you've ever committed to watch you wallow in self-pity and self-condemnation. He died so that you might be free. So that you, too, can conquer. For we are more than conquerors in Christ Jesus, and nothing can separate us from His love (my paraphrase; see Rom. 8:37–39). No matter what you face, no matter how loud your anxious thoughts roar and cripple, you are a conqueror. You are a warrior—not a worrier. And you have the supernatural strength of the Creator to overcome. You just have to reach out and ask for it. Grab it. Take it.

He wants you to be free. To live an abundant life. But you can't under the burden and angst of condemnation. It has been removed. So release it. Untangle your grip. Let go and live *free*.

You are a warrior— not a worrier.

Jesus, help me choose freedom. Sometimes I feel unworthy or undeserving. But You paid an extraordinary price for my freedom, and I want to accept it. I had assumed that my freedom came with salvation, and while I'm free from sin and death, I know now that I must choose to *live* in freedom. I can't do that on my own. Help me to harness the supernatural strength within me so that I can be a warrior for You, a conqueror that glorifies Your name. Amen.

CHALLENGE

Give yourself grace. Be gentle to yourself. Write down your rules, the belief system you live by, and compare those beliefs to how God desires you to live.

23

STEADFAST

You will keep in perfect peace him whose mind is steadfast,
because he trusts in you.
—Isaiah 26:3

An anxious mind is a flurry of activity. It darts from thought to thought at intense speeds, traveling from point A to point B without taking in the details of the journey. It's disjointed, distracted, divided.

Worry isn't slow—it's fast. It's busy. It keeps you moving but gets you nowhere.

The anxious mind does not know peace. It can't. Worry and peace never end up in the same room. Like a ball rolling down a hill, once anxiety begins to move within your heart, the decent into worry appears inevitable. Your mind travels faster and faster into the depths of despair and depression and uncertainty. All of which can have a devastating effect on your health. You can't focus. Your productivity slows. Your energy is sapped. You sleep too much, or maybe too little. Your head aches. You're wrought with nausea, and your muscles are tight.

Worry isn't slow—it's fast. It's busy. It keeps you moving but gets you nowhere.

God engrained a fight or flight response within each of us. This intense, emotional arousal sends adrenaline pumping through our veins, propelling us away from an oncoming car or from the edge of a steep cliff. It's an indispensible emotion in detecting danger and, in those instances, is natural. Normal. And quite frankly, beneficial.[1]

But God did not design us to sprint all day, every day. The fight or flight response was designed to be turned on and off. For someone prone to anxiety, that switch is stuck in the "on" position. You're constantly on the lookout for impending danger, even taking on the cares and concerns of others.

No wonder you are tired: you've been perpetually on the run.

The prophet Isaiah writes that we will keep in perfect peace when our minds are steadfast in Christ. The word "steadfast" is a verb, not a condition or state of being.[2] It's active. Our minds must continually be upheld, sustained, and rooted in Jesus Christ. And we must also allow Jesus to continually uphold and sustain our minds. When our minds and thoughts are fixated on Christ, we will be kept—preserved—in perfect peace. Tranquility, rest, peace . . . it all comes from God. Yet so often we try to manufacture it ourselves. It simply won't work. Any replica or knock-off version will be far from perfect.

> **Tranquility, rest, peace . . . it all comes from God. Yet so often we try to manufacture it ourselves. It simply won't work. Any replica or knock-off version will be far from perfect.**

In Hebrew, "perfect peace" is literally translated "peace, peace."[3] This repetition emphasizes the certainty and continuance of that peace. It's whole, it's complete, it's undisturbed. But in order to drink in abundant peace, you must submit your mind, and everything that comes from within, at the foot of the cross.

This verse holds promise. Wherever your mind is steadfast is where you'll find your trust. If your mind is steadfast on finances, your trust is in your finances. If your mind is steadfast on your job, you've placed your trust in your job. But if your mind is steadfast, fixated, and established upon the promises of Christ, your trust is rooted in Him.

At the end of the day, the presence of worry is misplaced faith. You have faith in something when you're worrying, but it's not faith in Christ.

You have faith in something when you're worrying, but it's not faith in Christ.

"Peace, peace," Isaiah says. As F. B. Meyer noted, if one assurance of peace is not enough (and it's often not for the fragile soul), God will follow that assurance with a second and a third.[4] He will steady your heart. That's the beauty of grace.

Jesus is the author of peace. The sustainer of peace. The Prince of Peace (see Isa. 9:6). Second Timothy 1:7 (KJV) says, "For God hath not given us a spirit of fear; but of power, and of love, and of a sound mind."

Do not call yourself a worrier. Don't say "I just can't help it." Don't call yourself an anxious person. There's a big difference between feeling and struggling with anxious thoughts and being ruled by them. Living in anxiousness, or worrying, is not part of your heavenly inheritance. It may have woven its way through your lineage, but you can stop the madness. Because that's what worry is—madness.

Remember, anxiety distracts and divides. In the New Testament, "anxiety" literally means to pull apart. Whereas "peace" means to join together. Polar opposites.[5]

You were given a sound mind. A peaceful mind. First Corinthians 2:16 says, "we have the mind of Christ." We are influenced by the power of the Holy Spirit. We are also influenced by the enemy. Both are vying for our attention and our thoughts. It's spiritual warfare. You can't give your worries to God with one hand and hold onto them with the other. It requires complete soul-surrendering. Open hands, held high to the Master.

"Peace, peace," He whispers. Can you hear Him reassuring you, coaxing you to let go and trust Him? Just trust Him.

> **You can't give your worries to God with one hand and hold onto them with the other.**

Peace is waiting on the other side.

Father, take my fears, my worries, and my anxieties. You've given me a sound mind—not a spirit of fear. That's from the enemy. Overwhelm me with Your perfect peace. I desperately want to put my trust in You. Keep my mind steadfast on Your promises. I can't wait to experience Your peace. Your perfect peace. Your enduring peace. Thank You, Father. Amen.

CHALLENGE

I think it's time you put your foot down. It's time you remind the enemy who is Lord over your life. I pray a righteous anger is smoldering in your soul when you realize how much the enemy has stolen from you. If God didn't give you a spirit of fear, but a sound mind, where did worry come from? The enemy. I've said it several times: he knows he can't have your soul, so he'll poison your mind with doubt, worry, and paralyzing panic to keep you from influencing the world for Christ. That's first-degree armed robbery. He's stolen your time and your energy. He's sapped the joy from your relationships. He's convinced you that you're a *worrier* when God calls you a *warrior*. His lies have seeped deep beneath your skin and penetrated your heart.

Pray with conviction today. Maybe you've excused your worry, nurtured it, denied it, or babied it. I did, too. God strengthened my heart slowly so that I could stand firm and put the enemy in his place. Don't allow the enemy to steal another moment, another hour. Cut him off. And if you pray and anxiety lingers, pray again and again and again. No one said it was easy—but I promise it's worth it. When your prayers come loud and firm and tough, when they reek with earnest conviction . . . those are the ones that scare the enemy. Shore up your heart with the promises of Christ. And stand firm on them.

24

YOKES

It is for freedom that Christ has set us free. Stand firm, then, and do not let yourselves be burdened again by a yoke of slavery.
—Galatians 5:1

Two oxen, cement blocks in tow, move forward—together, kicking up dust, as a whip slaps the dry ground. They grunt—tight, flexed muscles rippling beneath their skin. Wet, heavy breaths shake their nostrils as the firm voice of their master urges them on. Forward. Pull.

The two beasts are shackled together with a yoke—a wooden beam that binds them together to ensure they march forward in a straight line. Should one of them turn left or right, or even turn his head, the team's progression immediately halts. They must move together as a team, or not move forward at all.

The rules are simple: the oxen must pull in one continuous motion. As soon as the sled of cement stops moving for a fraction of a second, the round ends. No pause. No rest for the weary animals.

Then the judge measures the distance traveled, and the oxen's chains are released.

As spring melts into summer, county fairs start popping up throughout the state. Most New Englanders can testify to attending several of these historic events; others have made them an annual tradition. I grew up attending the county fair, riding the Ferris wheel, and indulging in sticky cotton candy and greasy fried dough. It's an old-fashioned summertime festivity that carries well into October, just before winter settles over the region.

Salvation doesn't propel or force you into a life of abundant living.

Oxen pulling is just one of the many agricultural events that is still demonstrated at the county fair. Along with horse pulls, sheep shearing, and woodsman competitions.

As a child, I was quite bored with the antics, not understanding why folks would cheer for oxen that dragged a few blocks of cement.

But today, I see such spiritual significance in it.

As I've journeyed down the slippery, treacherous, dark road to healing, I've grappled with the concept of "freedom in Christ." I believed freedom came packaged with salvation. But salvation doesn't propel or force you into a life of abundant living. No, that takes additional heart surgery. Salvation saves your soul, pulling it out of the clutches of the enemy. You become a member of Christ's family. You are His. Although salvation immediately frees you from the penalty of sin, *living* in freedom takes time and practice and diligence post-saving.

Until now, this idea was foreign to me.

Watching those oxen heave and sweat and buckle under the weight of that cement brought to life the words in Galatians 5.

While the oxen-pulling contests demonstrate great power, strength, and teamwork, it also paints of vivid picture of a life lived bound to our past, to our worry, and to our sin.

Jesus paid an exorbitant price for our salvation. He put on human skin and came to live among us, not so that we could live a life of mediocrity, but so that we could live of life of abundance (see John 10:10). That's an invitation from the mouth of Christ to accept a life brimming with promise and overflowing with His goodness.

> **Worry is looking Jesus in the eye and saying, "*I* can handle it. *I* can take care of it . . . I. Don't. Need. You."**

That's why He came.

To save us. To free us. To release us from the yoke of the Old Testament law, as Paul refers to in Galatians.[1] From the yoke of condemnation. From the yoke of flawless living. From the yoke of worry.

And while He lifted those yokes and released our chains so that we can run free and far, more often than not, we still operate under the yoke of worry, willingly placing the expectations of the world, our success or failure, on our feeble shoulders. I've often convinced myself that this terrible burden has been inflicted on me. That I'm a victim.

But if I were to look at my worry through the holy lens of God, I'd hide my face. As Eve did. As Adam did.

Why? Because worry is sin. Worry is pride. Worry is looking Jesus in the eye and saying, "*I* can handle it. *I* can take care of it . . . I. Don't. Need. You."

At the heart of worry is an overwhelming sense of self-reliance. By no means am I discounting the physical and psychological factors. Those remain. Like any disease or ailment, anxiety disorders require the same type of medical care. However, what I *am* saying is that we have more control over our thought patterns than we think.

The key to "controlling" worry is to release control over it.

I often think about my worry as a rabid, vicious dog pulling at the leash and gnashing its teeth. I fear that if I were to let go, the dog would run rampant through the house, tearing up carpets, dismantling my life, and ripping my thoughts from their unstable, flimsy hinges.

> **The key to "controlling" worry is to release control over it.**

The outcome is messy at best. It's risky. It's counterintuitive. I'd rather cling to the leash, blisters bursting beneath my skin, and hold on. To protect myself. To protect others.

But the key is to lean heavily on Christ . . . and let go.

We've seen this time and time again throughout Scripture. When Peter fixed his eyes on Jesus, he walked on water. When the disciples woke Jesus in the boat, the storm ceased.

Oxen shackled to a yoke can only look forward. They have tunnel vision. They move slowly, if at all, when shackled to their loads. The sharp crack of a whip and the loud voice of their master urges them forward. They're chained, slaves to the task. And while they can move, they are limited to their own strength.

But Christ's yoke is easy, His burden, light (see Matt. 11:30). Through Jesus' obedience on the cross, the yoke meant for us is no longer ours to bear. It's been replaced by an easy load that requires just one thing: acceptance.

And should we choose to accept, the penalty of sin is immediately removed, and we no longer have to operate under a yoke of worry. Like a prisoner acquitted of his crimes. His shame erased from the records. The shackles removed, free to make a fresh start.

But don't you see? There's a second choice to be made.

What if the prisoner never left his cell? He's been handed his freedom, yet stays in the "safety" of his prison. If this is what he chooses, is he still a free man?

Well, yes.

But is he really free? I'd argue no. Because he has returned to the yoke of bondage—he is living as though defined by the past. He isn't really free until he sheds the orange jumpsuit and walks out of the prison, across the street, and into new life.

Only then does freedom transpire into abundant living.

Jesus, it never occurred to me that while I may be free, I'm not living free. That I'm a free prisoner who won't leave his jail cell. Too often I've made my past, my mistakes, my failures, and my worry part of my identity. And until I let that go, I know that I won't find true freedom. I'm asking that You go before me today, that You guide me out of my cell and into *abundant living*. Clothe me in Your goodness, Your grace. Teach me how to live as You lived. And keep me from returning to my yoke of slavery and bondage. My freedom does not rest in self-righteous rules,

but in what You accomplished on the cross. I want to trade my yoke for Yours, Jesus. Thank You for an easy yoke. Thank You for a light burden. Thank You for removing the heavy and overwhelming yoke of the law and the yoke of worry. You are good, God. You are merciful and gracious. Thank You. Amen.

CHALLENGE

Healing requires constant self-examination. It requires taking a daily inventory. Ask yourself: am I still residing in my cell? That's a hard question to answer. But perhaps today the lights flickered on, and you realized where you've been living. The prison you felt trapped in has been unlocked the entire time . . . you just had to swing open the door and walk past the chain-linked fence. I pray you walk through it today.

25

CAST

Humble yourselves, therefore, under God's mighty hand, that he may lift you up in due time. Cast all your anxiety on him because he cares for you.
—1 Peter 5:6–7

A splintered tree, weathered and raw, rose up toward the sky before falling into the crimson ground. The tree swayed, the creaking of leather hides stretching beneath with the weight of His splitting flesh. And then, for a moment . . . stillness.

There He hung, an innocent King, hanging limp between two thieves.

The cross was bare, open. On display for gawkers to surround and mock. Even then, despite the searing torment and writhing pain, He forgives. Even though His accusers had no remorse in their souls.

Jesus shouldered the burden of sin that day and was forsaken by His Father. Is there no greater suffering, no greater agony than to have God's face turn from you? And yet, as He died on our behalf, your face and mine were surely at the forefront of His mind, making the excruciating pain worth it.

Because Jesus willingly climbed onto the cross, we never have to fear God turning away from us. We never have to experience the sheer emptiness and abandonment that Christ felt—because God sees us through the eyes of His Son.

It's a mesmerizing picture of grace. A gift unlike any other. And even after our debt is forgiven, we are invited to accept a continuous outpouring of His love. It's a gift that keeps on giving. "Cast all your anxiety on him," we read. The word "anxiety" is translated *merimna*. It encompasses anxieties, worries, and even concerns.[1] It's a noun. Scripture tells us to cast our feelings—before they turn into active worry—onto the bruised shoulders of our Savior. Cast them. Every last one of them. Throw them. With muscles pulsing under the inexpressible weight, push them out, away, from your chest and *onto* Him. Because He *cares* for you with such tenderness. He *adores* you.

He already shouldered your worries—past, present, and future—when He hung from that tree. When you don't throw your cares to Jesus, you're effectively trying to remove those burdens from His flogged, tired shoulders and put them on your own.

But you can't.

You aren't relieving Him of pain. You aren't lightening His load.

You are discrediting His sacrifice.

Before we can cast our cares, we must humble ourselves before Christ. We must surrender every thought, every will, to God. It takes deep reverence and submission. But His hand is mighty and in the midst of every situation and trouble.

The word for "hand" in this instance, *cheir*, can also mean power or control.[2] And friend, His power and control are *mighty*. His power is fierce. His control dependable.

Wouldn't you rather live under His mighty, powerful hand than under the heavy, burdensome hand of worry?

First Peter 5:7 says, "Cast all your anxiety . . ." Oh, how it requires a terrible exertion of energy at times. A deep exhale. A thrust toward something else.

How, then, do we cast cares?

> **And friend, His power and control are *mighty*. His power is fierce. His control dependable.**

Peter is echoing the call in Psalm 55:22, "Cast your cares on the LORD and he will sustain you; he will never let the righteous fall." Peter assures those he is writing to, once more, that they can trust God. They can let go. And so can we. When we do, God will sustain, He will provide, He will endure, and He will bear our anxieties. Why? Because He *cares* for us.

When you share a secret, confess a care, hand your child to another human being, you are saying with your actions that you trust that individual. You would never hand your infant to a stranger while you carried the groceries into your home. You wouldn't give your wedding band to a stranger for safekeeping. Nor would you give a passerby the keys to your home and ask them to feed your cats while you are out of town.

But you *would* do those things if you trusted that person. You would hand your child to your mother, trusting her to tenderly care for him while you ran errands. You would trust your spouse to hold on to your wedding ring while you underwent surgery. And you would hand your best friend the keys to your home, trusting she would care for your pets and water your plants.

So do you trust God? Can you hand Him your worries, turn around, and walk the other way? If you hand them over, will you keep an eye on God, making sure He doesn't accidently drop those worries? Forget about them?

He hungered to give you freedom. Freedom not just from the penalty of sin and death, but from *yourself*.

God isn't careless, friend. He isn't forgetful. He isn't scatterbrained. Fear is absolutely linked to our capacity to trust.

Trust Him.

As He struggled up the hill, to the place His Father had destined Him, I believe He saw your face. He kept moving because He knew you. He saw you. He ached to give you relief from worry. He hungered to give you freedom. Freedom not just from the penalty of sin and death, but from *yourself*.

Let Him carry you. He carried the splintered cross that was covered in your shame, your worry, your fear, and He defeated it.

He defeated it.

He defeated it.

Don't let those words hang light. Let them hang heavy over your heart. Release your worries. Whatever strength it takes to lay them at the foot of the cross, do it.

Father, thank You. Thank You for sending Your Son to the cross on my behalf. That cross was mine. It should have worn my flesh. But it doesn't have to now. Help me cast my worries and anxieties

onto You. I trust You, but I know that my actions often say that I don't. I want that to change. I want to live free, the way You intended. I want to show others, through my testimony, that there is freedom in Christ. And freedom in abundance. No matter what it takes, no matter how much strength, I pray You will intercede and release these worries from my weary heart. Take them. I trust You. Amen.

CHALLENGE

Someone once asked me if I trusted God, and my instinct, my flesh, said "yes." Yes, I do. Yes, I have. Yes, I always will. But if an outsider were to look only at my actions, they would probably say I didn't trust Him fully. That I trusted Him with some, but not with all.

Go for a walk today. Perhaps it's a bright, sunny day. Breathe it in. Maybe you have to slide on boots and tromp through the snow— look past the slush and toward the beauty of the untouched fallen snow. Settle your heart. And then, in the quiet, search it. Don't be afraid of what you'll find there. It's okay to say you don't trust God. Confess it. After all, you must recognize that first in order to begin fully trusting. Ask yourself why. For me, I discovered that I didn't trust anyone. Because too often, I was let down. So I built walls up around my heart and, as a result, saw God in the same light as those who weren't trustworthy. I placed human qualities onto a supernatural God, assuming His actions would mirror those of my friends, my boss, my coworkers, my family. It took some deep soul-searching to realize that while I trusted Him with most, I didn't trust him with all. He wanted my whole heart. My whole being. He wants yours, too. After all, a fragile soul is best handled by the Maker's hands. There is no safer place to be.

26

GUARD

Be self-controlled and alert. Your enemy the devil prowls around like a roaring lion looking for someone to devour.
—1 Peter 5:8

The cool, crisp air rolled over my skin, seeping through my thin layers. I tilted my chin toward the sky, dark and gray, heavy clouds hovering over the parking lot, threatening to burst. The days were getting shorter, the nights colder. One season passing the other.

The day looked weary and worn, but for the first time in months, my hands weren't quivering. My heart wasn't racing. My feet weren't rushing to the car, eager to escape. They were walking slow, light. A smile cracked my dry skin.

But something was wrong.

I drove home, hands tight on the steering wheel. Waiting. I got all the way to the traffic light. Paused. Waited. Turned left on green. Drove down the ramp. Merged onto the highway. Still waiting.

Nothing.

I drove past the tolls, kept left at the fork, and kept driving until my car came to a stop in my driveway.

I got out of the car, collected my belongings, and went inside. Something wasn't right. Something was off. Something was . . .

I went to the sink. Dishes piled high, neglected. My back to the door, hands buried deep in stainless steel and soapy water. I heard the front door squeak open and the loud thud as it closed. Scrub, scrub, scrub.

Tall, sweet, handsome husband came to my side, whispered hello. My hands were covered in soap and my brow sketched with deep lines.

"I'm not thinking about it," I said as I continued to scrub. That smile, that same smile from earlier, creased my cheeks.

"About what?" he asked.

"About work." I paused and looked up from the sink and into his face.

He stopped, letting the words hit him. "That's great!" he said.

"Just give it a couple hours," I replied, laughing it off.

That was it. That's what seemed "wrong": I wasn't thinking. My thoughts weren't whirring. My mind wasn't critiquing every move, every decision of the day. I wasn't second-guessing myself, doubting my capabilities. The feeling was so foreign that I hadn't been able to identify it. It felt so unfamiliar, so peculiar. So . . . so *good*.

But I quickly convinced myself that it was only a matter of time until the onslaught of anxiety would make its way into my evening and morph into worry that would last until I surrendered my body to sleep.

But it didn't. Not yet, anyway. Was this victory? Was this healing? Had I made it?

I curled up on the couch, popcorn in hand. My husband was on one end of the couch, I on the other, the next episode of our latest TV series binge ready to go. He turned off the lights, and I tossed a blanket over my legs.

That's when it happened. The thought. It got past the fortified walls.

Perhaps my hand hanging in mid-air between my popcorn bowl and my mouth, my gaze hovering over the edge of the coffee table, gave me away.

"What's wrong?" my husband asked, leaning in front of my stare, trying to break it.

I said nothing.

"What are you thinking about?"

"I told you," I sighed. "Just give it a couple hours."

In his playful way, he did his best to distract me, to get me to laugh at him, myself, the cat, anything.

I'm happy to say, it worked. That was two days ago, and today, well, I haven't thought too much about what could have or should have happened as I typically do.

I had tasted freedom. Like being trapped in a dark, ominous hole and seeing light for the first time, I squinted, not sure of what was happening. What was right looked so wrong, and what was wrong looked so right.

And I learned a powerful lesson that day. One that I've known my whole life, but hadn't really identified until that moment: The enemy attacks when the lights go down. When the world gets quiet. When the sky turns black.

When we enter the safety of our homes, we tend to let our guard down. We ease into a nighttime routine, curling up and resting from the day's toil. That's when he strikes. When we are most susceptible to his deceit. When we are weak and tired. When we're hungry. That's when he engages our minds. He's crafty and sneaky and conniving.

We must be vigilant even when we think the temptation to worry has passed. Yes, you should rest in the peace of Jesus Christ. But you shouldn't draw back your forces. Stay alert. Be on guard. After all, Peter used strong language in describing the enemy's tactics.

> **The enemy attacks when the lights go down. When the world gets quiet. When the sky turns black.**

"Your enemy the devil prowls around like a roaring lion looking for someone to devour," Peter writes. I've seen lions depicted on the covers of calendars. They lie peacefully in the grass, a sturdy, devout look in their eyes. King of the jungle. Lord of the land. And yet, if you've ever watched how the lion attacks his prey on one of those nature shows, you know that gentle giant isn't so gentle. He's fierce. He's brutal. And he takes no prisoners.

The word Peter uses for "prowls around" is *peripateō* which means to walk around, to live, or to conduct one's life.[1] The enemy doesn't prowl around for a bit and then lie in the grass to take a nap—he has made his prowling a way of life. He lurks in the shadows of your day, waiting to pounce. Waiting for your weakest moment.

He's always ready to attack. And not just to attack, but to *devour*. The word "devour," *katapinō*, means more than "eat." It can mean to swallow, to devour, to be overwhelmed or drowned.[2] He wants to annihilate you. And he doesn't just look around once or twice. He's *looking*: a continuous action.

This isn't meant to frighten you—it's meant to embolden you to take up your arms, shore up the walls around your mind, and barricade the gateway to your thoughts.

So be alert. Stay vigilant. Refresh your forces. You may have won a battle, but the enemy is still warring for your mind.

Words are powerful. When it occurred to me that I wasn't worrying for the first time in months, I made it a joke. I discredited the significance. And by doing so, I pulled back my forces, let down my guard, and allowed the enemy to sneak in unnoticed.

As you walk further down this road of recovery, staying alert and clear-headed has an even greater significance. Perhaps you've begun to win battles, and you're becoming a bit more confident. Don't allow that victory to be trampled on by the enemy. He sees your progress. He knows your heart is fighting for freedom. So be alert. Stay vigilant. Refresh your forces. You may have won a battle, but the enemy is still warring for your mind.

Heavenly Father, thank You for the good moments. Thank You for those times when I feel sane. For those times I am unafraid. Even if it's only for what feels like a fraction of second. Those are moments to be so grateful for, so thank You. But Lord, as I bask in the little victories, help me not forget that the enemy is still warring for my mind. Help me be strong and not grow weary. Protect me when the enemy tries to devour my mind at night. Reveal to me when I am most susceptible to the enemy's

attack so that I can stand ready. Amen.

CHALLEGE

I set alarms to remind me of various tasks. Tonight, I'm going to set a new alarm. Every night at 7:00 p.m., I want to be reminded about that lion—that creature—that sneaks in the backdoor of my mind. I don't want him to get by unnoticed, so I'm going to make sure 1 Peter 5:8 pops up on my phone at the same time every evening. I encourage you to do the same. Be alert. Fill your mind with Scripture, spend a portion of your evening in the Word, and be intentional about thinking on all that is pure, lovely, and pleasing to God (see Phil. 4:8).

27

WORSHIP

For although they knew God, they neither glorified him as God nor gave thanks to him, but their thinking became futile and their foolish hearts were darkened. Although they claimed to be wise, they became fools and exchanged the glory of the immortal God for images made to look like mortal man and birds and animals and reptiles. . . . They exchanged the truth of God for a lie, and worshipped and served created things rather than the Creator— who is forever praised. Amen.
—Romans 1:21–23, 25

My hands lifted high in complete surrender, palms open—inviting the presence of the Father into my broken heart; song like an anthem rang deep and heavy across the sanctuary, shaking the walls and causing the floor to tremble against the mighty sound of voice and instrument. The harmonies swept over my skin, washing me in the echo of worship. Men and women around me stood shoulder to shoulder, faces to the ceiling, eyes closed, swaying, rejoicing, weeping . . . worshipping. One collective voice filled the air, my own included, before the throne of grace. My soul totally immersed, completely present.

The music slowed, the hum of the guitar fading into quiet, and we were asked to find our seats. I sat, legs crossed and arms folded, intent on the teaching to follow. Several minutes passed, and then, like a sudden impact, God pierced my heart with undeniable, earth-shattering truth. It's as if He were sitting across from me, face to face, His eyes holding mine. The words—His words—were so bold, so compelling and convicting, it's as if they were spoken aloud, colliding with my soul and sending the congregation into unceremonious silence.

Where your worry is, there your worship is also.

I distinctly remember my eyes growing wide, keenly aware that I had just heard the voice of God speak into my heart.

I scrambled through my purse, looking for a pen. The words kept coming, like a rising tide, swelling my mind with what was, moments ago, unknown to my soul.

Where your worry is, there your worship is also.

Those sitting in the row in front of me shifted in their seats.

I searched a bit more quietly; however, it was like I swimming to the surface of the ocean, nearly out of breath, my lungs burning. I needed to get the words He was giving me on paper before they were forever lost.

At last, I found a red marker at the bottom of my tote bag and snatched the tithe envelope from the chair in front of me. The words came in a fury.

All this time, all these months, all these years, I had found my control, my sanity, in worry. And yet, it drove me simultaneously to insanity. While I scribbled down the words as they came to my mind, I began to ask myself, *Where is my worry? Where? Where did I place it? Where do I let it rent space in my head?*

God's space had shrunk to no more than a closet-sized box, while worry resided in the main living quarters. My Savior had become more of a safety net than a reigning King.

It didn't take long. God was intent on giving me many answers that day. *Work*, He said. *Your job. Your success. Your performance.* I worshipped that cubical. I saw that office chair as my throne. I worried about work *at* work. I worried about work at home. I dreamt about work at night. I worried on my drive to the office. About making a mistake. About failing my boss, my coworkers, the company at large. I spent so much energy worrying that it sapped my joy dry.

The space in my mind that was once held exclusively for my Savior was being rented out to worry. Without me even noticing, God's space had shrunk to no more than a closet-sized box, while worry resided in the main living quarters. My Savior had become more of a safety net than a reigning King.

I shuddered.

Worship is part of who we are. We're designed for worship. It's in our makeup. But the enemy is crafty, cunning, and manipulative, and he can lead us to turn worship, which is meant exclusively for Christ, toward something else in an instant.

In that moment, I realized that I worshipped my performance. But I was only able to figure that out by evaluating *what I spent the most time worrying about.*

The object of my worry became my idol. And my idol secured my worship.

What are you worshipping?

I ask this not to condemn you, but to free you. Because as soon as you identify what has secured your worship, you can put it back in its rightful place and turn your worship back to Christ, where it rightfully belongs.

You see, back in the day, idols were made of wood and stone and precious metals. They were physical creatures erected for praise and adoration. But what is an idol, really? It's anything that pulls our attention and devotion away from Christ.

> **I glorified my own strength—rather than what God's strength was capable of doing *through* me. That exchange of worship is lethal to the human heart.**

I was devoted to worry. I was a *slave* to its demands.

It wasn't until God spoke those powerful words into my heart— *where your worry is, your worship is also*—that I realized I was robbing *Him* of true worship and robbing *myself*, consequently, of His true peace.

I, like the Roman church, had exchanged the truth for a lie. I exchanged the worship of God for the worship of worry. And where was my worry? I placed it in performance, in my work. And ultimately worshipped it. I glorified my own strength—rather than what God's strength was capable of doing *through* me. That exchange of worship is lethal to the human heart.

I served worry by becoming a slave to it. I succumbed to the onslaught of thoughts. I entertained fears of failure. I honored worry with my time. I harbored it in my heart. And I welcomed it, on occasion, too afraid, too tired to reject it. Ultimately, I meditated on those seeds of worry until they grew up into intense fear and dread, creating roots of a disorder in my heart. I did all this instead of meditating on the grace and power of Jesus Christ.

Where your worry is, your worship is also.

Where is your worship today?

Father, I never recognized that worry could easily morph into an idol. I never connected the dots—until today. Help me crush that idol of worry. When I take my anxious thoughts and indulge them, those fears infest my mind and break out into worried habits. Lord, I see now that when that happens, worry becomes my god. Whether I want it to be or not. Satan's crafty that way. Thank You for revealing that to me today. Give me energy, strength, and determination to put worry where it belongs and You back in Your rightful place. I love You, Jesus. Forgive me for putting worry on the throne. Set me free from the bondage of my thoughts and give me the discipline to take every thought captive. Amen.

CHALLENGE

Several chapters ago, I asked you to write down what triggered your anxiety—what caused it to creep in unannounced. Go back to that list today. What's the thread that binds all of those triggers together? For me, it's performance. I encourage you to identify where your worry is so you can turn your worship back to Jesus.

28

DISCOVER

There was given me a thorn in my flesh, a messenger of Satan, to torment me. Three times I pleaded with the Lord to take it away from me. But he said to me, "My grace is sufficient for you, for my power is made perfect in weakness." Therefore, I will boast all the more gladly about my weaknesses, so that Christ's power may rest on me. That is why, for Christ's sake, I delight in weaknesses, in insults, in hardships, in persecutions, in difficulties. For when I am weak, then I am strong.
—2 Corinthians 12:7–10

There's a green checkered chair in her office. Big, plush, inviting. It's a small room, just enough space for a couple chairs and a desk, but she made it homey with soft colors and warm light. I had sat in that chair every Monday morning for months. I'd plop my purse on the floor, curl my calves up underneath my thighs pretzel-style, and lean heavily on the thick arm of the chair, coffee in hand. She always met me with a smile, even at such an early-morning hour. And we'd talk. Dissecting my past, my present. It had been nearly eleven months since we first met, and I guess, at that point, I had expected a breakthrough. Some clarity. Some form of healing. Relief.

Anxiety disorders are a lot of work. It takes a team of profession-als—she was, and still is, one of them. She's my therapist, my counselor, my cheerleader, my challenger, my tell-me-what-I-need-to-hear-even-if-it-hurts accountability partner. She confronts the lies my thoughts produce. She helps me face unspeakable fear. And she walked me through the first few months, as if holding my hand, when anxiety held me captive, starving me of peace, hope, joy—anything remotely good.

Our journey together had started the day after Thanksgiving, and here we were, nearly a year later, the fall foliage at its peak.

That morning is one I'll never forget. October 13. Columbus Day. A day of *discovery*. I sank into that chair, one question burning in my mind: *If God promises freedom, then why hasn't He freed me from this? Why hasn't He taken it away? I've done everything I know to do. I've surrendered over and over and over. But I'm not free . . . why?*

I was afraid of the answer. Afraid that His promise would fall flat. We sat with that question for a while. We muddled over it, exam-ining it from all sides. And she planted seeds into my heart. Seeds that couldn't burst forth with life in a forty-five-minute window. But they had been planted, nonetheless.

---

*My freedom isn't necessarily freedom from your anxiety disorder . . . it's freedom from being a **slave to it.***

I got up, walked through her office door, down the stairs, and to my car.

I had a lot to think about. A lot to pray about.

Little did I know that God was about to open my eyes right then and there. As I drove, I felt Him nudging my heart. And just like that moment in church when He revealed to me that my worry and my worship lived in the same room, these words hit me just as intensely: *Samantha, My freedom isn't necessarily freedom from your anxiety disorder . . . it's freedom from being a **slave to it.***

Had I not been on Interstate 95, I would have slammed on my brakes and pulled over to catch my breath.

There was a swelling in my heart; those seeds were springing forth with life renewed. And then suddenly, truth, like a waterfall, came pouring over my soul.

Somewhere, deep down in the recesses of my heart, I had believed that if I had enough faith, anxiety would disappear. That if I did everything *right*, God would bless me by eradicating anxiety from my life.

But that wasn't it at all.

As I was driving home, Jesus reminded me of the apostle Paul, and how he was plagued by a thorn in his side that never let up, never went away. It tormented him day and night, even though he had dedicated his life to serving Christ. We don't know what that thorn was, but we do know that no amount of faith relieved him of it. It was a burden, a cross he had no choice but to bear.

But while he bore that cross, *Jesus* carried *him*.

Paul asked the Lord three times to take away the thorn. He pleaded, he begged. This thorn, whatever it was, tortured him.

I can imagine Paul on his knees before the heavens, arms outstretched, begging aloud, "Please take this from me, God. Please remove this pain, this affliction, this torment." His pleas sound eerily similar to my own. Do they echo your heart's cries as well?

In 2 Corinthians 12:7, the Greek word for "torment" can mean "to strike with the fists, beat, torment."[1] Isn't that what anxiety does? It hits us when we're down. It's rabid, throwing fists and creating welts that are felt long after the panic subsides, weakening its victim to the core. And like a thorn or a splinter, it's always nagging, always present, never easing.

It's no wonder Paul *begged* for relief.

Over and over again, Scripture tells us that God is our refuge, our strength, our rest, our support, our hope, and our help (see Ps. 46:1; Matt. 11:28–30; and Ps. 18:18, 25:5). He gives us rest—in the *midst* of trouble. He gives us peace—in the *heart* of the storm. He gives us strength—in the *middle* of unspeakable turmoil.

While complete deliverance and healing are absolutely possible through Christ, more often than not we read how God rides out the storm *with* us, choosing not to eradicate our strife but giving us the strength and endurance to withstand it.

But why?

To be honest, we may never know. What we *do know* is that the Lord's grace is sufficient. His power is made perfect in our weakness.

In what weakness? The allure of sin and temptation? Sure. In persecution and suffering? (see 2 Cor. 11:24–28). Of course. But the Greek word Paul uses for "weakness," *astheneia*, can also mean illness or infirmity.[2] Paul could very well have been pleading for relief from an illness—like yours, like mine.

I'm reminded of the blind man that Jesus and the disciples encountered in John 9. When they passed the man who had been blind since birth, the disciples asked, "Rabbi, who sinned, this man or his parents, that he was born blind?" And Jesus replied, "Neither this man nor his parents sinned, but *this happened so that the work of God might be displayed in his life*" (v. 2–3, emphasis mine).

The blind man was healed. Paul was not. But *both* men were used to glorify Jesus Christ. One was no more important than the other (see Rom. 2:11). Jesus cared deeply for them both; however, He was, and still is, far *more* concerned with the Father's will.

If you allow God to work through your weakness, your illness, your thorn, He could use you to make indispensable progress for the kingdom.

And Paul's weakened human condition was the perfect backdrop for Him to demonstrate His divine power.[3]

Your thorn, my thorn, is an opportunity for God to do the same. If you allow God to work through your weakness, your illness, your thorn, He could use you to make indispensable progress for the kingdom.

Because His power is made complete within you, you can rise above the worry. You no longer have to be a slave to it. You can discover, as I have, how to stand over it as David stood over Goliath, victorious. Anxiety may rise up strong at times and circumvent the troops you have guarding your heart and mind, but through the power of Christ, you can overcome. You can take that thought captive and make it obedient to the Word of God (see 2 Cor. 10:5). That's Christ's power *in* you.

And because Christ's power is within you, you are *free* (see 2 Cor. 3:17). Free from slaving under worry's demands. Free to utilize the full power of Christ.

Don't be discouraged if you're still struggling. When anxiety swells up in your heart or comes barreling down on you, remember that you have the power to stand and to *with*stand whatever comes your way.

Freedom isn't always the absence of anxiety, it's learning to live above it through the power of Christ.

Heavenly Father, like Paul, I've often begged You to take this affliction away, to eradicate crippling anxiety from my life. Help me see that Your grace is sufficient. I do not have to be a slave to worry because I am free in You. I don't have to listen to its demand because Your strength and power are made complete, whole, and perfect in my weakness. Help me bring fame not to my struggle, but to Your supernatural strength in the *midst* of my struggle. I want people to have no choice but to point to You. I want You to be glorified in every aspect of my life—even my emotional distress. Use my life, my thorn, to show others Your grace. Amen.

CHALLENGE

Have you questioned the goodness of Christ because your prayers for deliverance seem to go unanswered? Have you doubted His sufficiency? Remember: freedom isn't always the absence of anxiety; it's learning to live above it through the power of Christ. *That's* deliverance. Write down 2 Corinthians 12:9 in your journal today: "My grace is sufficient for you, for my power is made perfect in weakness." Memorize it. There is power in meditating on God's Word and committing Scripture to memory. When Satan tries to get you to question the goodness of your Savior, recite these words aloud. Fight him off with Scripture, just as Jesus did (see Matt. 4:1–11).

29

BOUNDLESS

I can do everything through him who gives me strength.
—Philippians 4:13

There's a man sitting in a bar, hoards of people around him, laughter, noise, steins spilling over with frothy foam. A recovered alcoholic, a man trying desperately to live sober. A man driven to pull his life together. He'd been going to AA, he was seeing his doctor to check in, and he was even seeing a counselor every other week.

But here he was—in a bar.

He meandered his way around tables, rubbing shoulders with the intoxicated, and found an unoccupied stool. Its legs scratched the pub floor as he pulled in close to the bar. And then he prayed, "Father, help me not to drink. Help me to withstand the urge to get drunk. Free me, Lord. Save me."

And so the man sat and waited. Within minutes, the bartender approached him, leaning heavily on his palms, "What'll it be?" he asked.

"Oh, I'm not here to drink," the man said.

The bartender looked at him, puzzled. "Want something to eat then?"

"No, no," the man replied. "I'd just like to sit awhile."

And so he sat and observed the chaotic scene. Every patron had a glass in hand—a beer, a martini, a fruity mixed drink. Some were throwing back shots, others were staring bleary-eyed at the band playing in the corner. The man kept praying, "God, You say I can do all things through Him who gives me strength. Give me the power to resist this. I'll know I'm recovered if I can sit here without getting drunk."

The bartender returned twenty minutes later and asked again, "So. What'll it be? Can I get you something to drink?

The man paused, conflicted. The bartender stood before him, eyes locked, waiting for a response. Anxiety surged in the man's chest. The bar was packed and he was taking up a valuable seat. Maybe I'll just have one, he thought. So long as I don't get drunk, I'm okay.

"I'll have a scotch," he replied. "On the rocks."

Three hours later, he's too far gone. The bartender called a cab, and the man went home.

The very next day, the man returned at happy hour. He walked in, pulled up a chair, and began to pray just as he had the day before. "God, You said I can do all things, so give me the strength to withstand temptation."

Once again, he failed.

He does this time and time and time again: going to the same place, praying the same prayer, and receiving the same result.

Isn't that the definition of insanity?

I have behaved the same way at times, purposely putting myself in tempting situations to test my strength. I believed, like the man in this story, that I had to withstand temptation in order to conquer temptation.

But by doing that, I was deliberately taking the reins, defining strength by what my flesh could accomplish, and disobeying God's call on my life.

Have you tested your own strength only to fail?

Philippians 4:13 says, "I can do everything through him who gives me strength." That was the verse the man in the story clung to. It's the verse I've clung to.

But did you know that many Bible commentaries actually say a more exact translation of this verse would be "I have strength for all things," or "I have strength in all things"?[1] Paul, writing from a prison, was able to *bear* the weight of the circumstances he was *placed* in—the situations that were out of his immediate control.

As Christians, we often cherry-pick the verses that sound the most promising, and Philippians 4:13 satisfies that need. It's a great bumper sticker. A great status update. But by examining the words that surround that verse, we see that it's part of a much greater thought:

"I am not saying this because I am in need, for I have learned to be content whatever the circumstances. I know what it is to be in need, and I know what it is to have plenty. I have learned the secret of being content in any and every situation, whether well fed or hungry, whether living in plenty or in want. I can do everything through him who gives me strength" (Phil. 4:11–13).

Jesus gives us strength to bear the unpredictable, to stand up under the weight of situations and tragedies that we cannot control.

We must put Scripture into context. If we were to take verse 13 by itself, it would mean that Paul could do all things without limitation. But he is not God and is therefore limited by the human condition. Rather, he was able to *endure* what he was unable to control. He was able to *bear* what He could not change, knowing that God had the power to change those circumstances if He chose to. But if He didn't, Paul would press on.

The context changes the meaning altogether.

Jesus gives us strength to bear the unpredictable, to stand up under the weight of situations and tragedies that we cannot control.

Paul, writing from a dark and damp first-century prison cell, isn't saying that we have the supernatural strength to do whatever we set our minds to, but rather that we can withstand everything we are *called to*. As author John Merritt writes, "He's not encouraging Christians to go out and conquer the world; he's reminding them that they can press on when the world conquers them."[2] It is not about self-sufficiency. It's about being content and faithful, regardless of what life brings *to* you.

Do not become disillusioned by Philippians 4:13. The enemy would love to twist Scripture and leave you wondering if you can really do "all things" through Christ. When you don't reach your goal, fulfill your dream, get the promotion, or bury a mental illness, he wants you to immediately question God's goodness. When, really, God is calling us to set up boundaries unique to our weakness so that we can live bound*less*.

We must yield to Christ, draw near to Him, and organize our lives in such a way that honors our Savior and makes us more effective for His kingdom. That isn't weak—that's *wise*.

For those who struggle with alcoholism, it probably means staying away from bars and pubs. It means keeping the cabinets free from alcohol. It means cutting off relationships with drinking buddies that don't support their quest for sobriety.

> **God is calling us to set up boundaries unique to our weakness so that we can live bound*less*.**

For me, and maybe for you, it's removing certain key words from my vocabulary. "Should," for instance, immediately puts me in the wrong mindset. As soon as I start "should-ing" myself, I catapult my anxious *thoughts* into worrisome *behavior. I should check that*, I think. *I shouldn't have said that.* And before I know it, I've "should" myself all the way into obsessive compulsions.

Set up boundaries in your life so you can bask in the true freedom of Jesus Christ.

James 4:7 says, "Resist the devil. . . ." We must play an active role in our recovery in order to live a free and abundant life. It doesn't happen unconsciously. We must stand firm. We must persevere and hold our ground. We must stay alert and attentive.

Don't give the enemy a chance to take you down. Draw a line in the sand. Fortify the walls around your heart so that you are not tempted to sit down and worry about all the things that may or may not happen. Resist him.

Strike up a rebellion. Stand firm on your faith. Actively participate in the war. Move up to the front lines.

Do whatever it takes.

Stop sitting in the "bar" while you're praying for healing.

Strike up a rebellion. Stand firm on your faith. Actively participate in the war. Move up to the front lines.

Heavenly Father, too often I cling to Bible verses that "sound good." Remind me to put Your Word and the words of others into context. With Your strength, I can keep the enemy from gaining a foothold in my mind. Continue to show me where I may have taken Your words out of context. Set me free with Your truth today, Father. Show me the areas in my life where I need to set up boundaries. Thank You for Your Word, Your truths, and Your promises. Thank You for Your goodness. Amen.

CHALLENGE

Do you "should" yourself often? Have you "what if'd" yourself straight into a panic attack? What words do you often recite subconsciously that you need to guard against in order to live boundless? Are there thought patterns that feed your anxiety? Behaviors that breed it? Have you surrendered your worry but refused to make the changes God has called you to make? Are you still sitting in the "bar"?

It's time to move up to the front lines. Identify boundaries that will help you avoid worried behavior. Here's what those boundaries might look like: choosing to evict words like "should" and phrases like "what if" from your vocabulary; scheduling your evenings because you know worry takes its stand when the lights go down and distractions are few; removing certain songs from your playlist because they cause unnecessary anxiety or flood you with memories of a past that's been forgiven. Spend time in prayer today and ask the Lord to show you how to set up boundaries so that you can live boundless in Him.

30

PEACE

"Peace I leave with you; my peace I give you. I do not give to you as the world gives. Do not let your hearts be troubled and do not be afraid."
—John 14:27

What a journey this has been. Hills and valleys, long highways, offbeat paths and detours, but here we are. We've crossed the finish line on our journey together, but I pray you continue to move forward on the hunt for whom God designed and called you to be. I pray you embrace the journey. The one that, perhaps, has only just begun. I pray you begin to share your story with others, as I have shared mine. This was such a humbling and transparent journey for me, but one that taught me that light and darkness cannot coexist. When we shed light on our struggles, the darkness has no choice but to flee. When we bring Christ into the equation, the enemy has no choice but to cower at His holiness.

When we bring Christ into the equation, the enemy has no choice but to cower at His holiness.

Although this was a tremendous struggle, part of my soul thanks God for it. Because it brought me to my knees before Christ.

That's where peace is.

How Jesus longs for us to walk in peace, the peace that surpasses all human understanding (see Phil. 4:7). Peace is His legacy, His parting gift, our inheritance.

Oh, to taste inner rest, total well-being, for just a moment this side of heaven.

And we can.

Jesus told his disciples that He was imparting peace. *His* peace. And He left us with the Holy Spirit, the spirit of truth, "the Counselor" who would administer that peace to us (see John 14:26). What a beautiful picture of God's gentleness and provision and grace.

"Peace I leave you" was a common Jewish phrase.[1] Jesus uses its familiarity as a segue. However, this was not an empty wish or salutation. It was a promise. A promise they could cling to well before He departed—

Peace is His legacy, His parting gift, our inheritance.

and long after as well. Jesus was already setting up provisions for them, caring for them, long before they knew the circumstances Jesus spoke of.

Peace. True peace. Not the peace that the world gives, but peace that comes from the one true God. The peace He sacrificed for. The peace that's possible because He so longed for reconciliation with His creation.

Peace is a gift. As if His dying wasn't enough, He not only offers salvation through His name, He imparts peace. Peace for now.

Not just peace somewhere on the other side of this life. Peace for all circumstances, all trials, all labors, all heartache.

He loves you. He loves you deeply, tremendously. If you are left with nothing else from this scattering of words, I pray you saw His love like fingerprints on the pages.

Jesus Christ has given you a spirit of peace that lives within you. Fear may swell up in your chest, but remember: if you are a child of God, peace already resides in your heart. For Jesus said, "On that day you will realize that I am in my Father, and you are in me, and I am in you" (John 14:20).

You do not have to be a slave to worry. You can choose to be free in Christ.

Anxiety will come upon your heart at times. Troubles will rise. Heartache will follow. But you don't have to be a slave to worry's demands. You can battle them with truth. You can choose to be a slave to righteousness.

Jesus left an inheritance of peace that is yours for the taking. Let Him be your Savior. Let Him love you. Let Him hold you. Let Him carry you as you carry your cross. And may the peace of Christ follow you into every tomorrow.

Jesus, You left behind peace when You departed the earth. You told us we had no reason to fear, no reason to be afraid. I am confident that You can saturate my thoughts with Your peace. I love You, Jesus. Thank You for being in the trenches with me. For never leaving my side. And for fighting on my behalf. Amen.

CHALLENGE

Rest . . . and then start writing your story.

Contact the Author

I would love to hear from you. Send a note to
fragile@samanthaarroyo.com, or visit my website at
www.samanthaarroyo.com.

DO YOU KNOW THE PRINCE OF PEACE?

True peace, whole peace, is not possible without knowing the Prince of Peace.

If you've read this book but haven't called on the name of the Lord, the peace you're seeking will go unfound. You can fight your anxiety and manage your worry, but if you don't have Someone to hand it to, you'll never be truly free. That Someone is Jesus. He is the only one who can break the chains of worry, who can remove the shackles of fear, who can unlock your cell door.

All you have to do is call on Him. That's it. Scripture says, "everyone who calls on the name of the Lord will be saved" (Joel 2:32; Acts 2:21; Rom. 10:13). It's a promise. It's a gift. And it's yours for the taking.

There's no special prayer you have to recite or formula you have to solve. You simply have to believe in your heart that He died for your sins and rose again, ask Him for forgiveness, and accept Him as Lord of your life. Romans 10:9–10 says, "If you confess with your mouth, 'Jesus is Lord,' and believe in your heart that God raised him from the dead, you will be saved. For it is with your heart that you believe and are justified, and it is with your mouth that you confess and are saved." Friend, you just need to accept the gift. I pray you do today.

Love,
Samantha

P.S. If you have questions or have accepted Jesus Christ as your Lord and Savior, write me at fragile@samanthaarroyo.com.

FRAGILE

ENDNOTES

"LETTER"
1. Edward W. Gregg et al., "Association of an Intensive Lifestyle Intervention With Remission of Type 2 Diabetes," JAMA Network, December 19, 2012, doi: 10.1001/jama.2012.67929. Also see Genevra Pittman, "Diabetes Remission Possible with Diet, Exercise," Reuters, http://www.reuters.com/article/2012/12/18/us-diabetes-remission-idUSBRE8BH18Z20121218.
2. Author used the NIV translation of the Bible for this research.

"FALL"
1. Edward W. Goodrick and John R. Kohlenberger III, *The Strongest NIV Exhaustive Concordance* (Grand Rapids, MI: Zondervan, 2004), 1421.

"WORRY"
1. Goodrick and Kohlenberger III, *Strongest Concordance*, 1576.
2. Ibid., 1536.

"HE WEPT"
1. Matthew Henry, "Text Commentaries: Matthew Henry (Blue Letter Bible: John)," Blue Letter Bible, last modified March 1, 1996, http://www.blueletterbible.org/Comm/mhc/Jhn/Jhn_011.cfm. See specific commentary for John 11:5–6.
2. *NIV Study Bible (Fully Revised) – Supplementary Materials* (Grand Rapids, MI: Zondervan, 2002), 1651–52.
3. Ibid., 1652.
4. Ibid.

"YOU"
1. *NIV – Supplementary Materials*, 1615.
2. Goodrick and Kohlenberger III, *Strongest Concordance*, 1524.

Also see "Greek Lexicon :: G74 (NIV)," Blue Letter Bible, accessed March 11, 2015, http://www.blueletterbible.org/lang/lexicon/lexicon.cfm?Strongs=G74&t=NIV.

3. Goodrick and Kohlenberger III, *Strongest Concordance*, 1546.

4. "Greek Lexicon :: G1617 (NIV)," Blue Letter Bible, accessed May 5, 2015, http://www.blueletterbible.org/lang/lexicon/lexicon.cfm?Strongs=G1617&t=NIV.

5. *NIV – Supplementary Materials*, 1903.

6. *NIV – Supplementary Materials*, 1616.

7. Dave Miller, "HEMATIDROSIS," 2010, Apologetics Press, accessed November 10, 2014, http://www.apologeticspress.org/apcontent.aspx?category=13&article=2323.

8. Goodrick and Kohlenberger III, *Strongest Concordance,* 1570.

"SUFFERING"

1. Matthew Henry, "Text Commentaries: Matthew Henry (Blue Letter Bible: Job)," Blue Letter Bible, http://www.blueletterbible.org/Comm/mhc/Job/Job_002.cfm. See specific commentary for Job 2:1–6.

"STORMS"

1. Robert Jamieson, A. R. Fausset, and David Brown, "Text Commentaries: Jamieson, Fausset & Brown (Blue Letter Bible: Mark)," Blue Letter Bible, last modified February 19, 2000, http://www.blueletterbible.org/Comm/jfb/Mar/Mar_004.cfm. See notes on verse 38.

2. Goodrick and Kohlenberger III, *Strongest Concordance,* 1601.

3. Goodrick and Kohlenberger III, *Strongest Concordance,* 1491.

"STILL"

1. "Luke 10:38–42 NIV," Bible Gateway, accessed March 31, 2015, https://www.biblegateway.com/passage/?search=luke+10%3A38-42&version=NIV.

"FEAR"

1. David Guzik, "Commentary on Judges 7:1," in "David Guzik Commentaries on the Bible," Studylight, http://www.studylight.org/commentaries/guz/view.cgi?book=jud&chapter=007. 1997–2003. See commentary on verses 2 and 3. (Text courtesy of BibleSupport.com; used by permission.)

2. See Charles Ellicott, "Judges 7," in "Ellicott's Commentary for English Readers," 1905, Bible Hub, March 12, 2015, http://biblehub.com/commentaries/ellicott/judges/7.htm.

"RESOLVE"

1. "Verses 1–13," in "2 Chronicles 20 – Matthew Henry Commentary," Bible Gateway, accessed March 13, 2015, https://www.biblegateway.com/passage/?search=2+Chronicles+20&version=NIV.

2. Ibid.

3. Lysa TerKeurst, "I Need a Procedure Manual," in *Unglued.* (Grand Rapids, MI: Zondervan, 2012), 108.

4. Ibid., 112.

"GOLIATH"

1. John Gill, "Commentary on 1 Samuel 17:1," in "The New John Gill's Exposition of the Entire Bible," http://www.studylight.org/commentaries/geb/view.cgi?bk=1sa&ch=17. 1999. See "Verse 4."

2. Jamieson, Fausset, and Brown, "Commentary on 1 Samuel 17:1" in "Commentary Critical and Explanatory on the Whole Bible," http://www.studylight.org/commentaries/jfb/view.cgi?bk=1sa&ch=17. 1871–78. Also see Adam Clarke, "Commentary on 1 Samuel 17:1," in "The Adam Clarke Commentary," Studylight, http://www.studylight.org/commentaries/acc/view.cgi?bk=1sa&ch=17. 1832. See "Verse 5" and "Verse 6."

3. *NIV – Supplementary Materials,* 401.

4. Max Lucado, "Facing Your Giants," *Facing Your Giants: A David and Goliath Story for Everyday People* (Nashville: W Group, a Divi-

sion of Thomas Nelson, 2006), 5. (Used by permission.)

"STAND"
1. Goodrick and Kohlenberger III, *Strongest Concordance,* 1411.
2. *NIV – Supplementary Materials*, 401–02.

"GAMES"
1. Ethelbert William Bullinger, "Commentary on 1 Samuel 17:16," in "E. W. Bullinger's Companion Bible Notes," Studylight, http://www.studylight.org/commentaries/bul/view.cgi?bk=1sa&ch=17. 1901–22. (Text courtesy of BibleSupport.com; used by permission.)

"NAME"
1. Matthew Henry, "1 Samuel 17:26–45 NIV," in "Matthew Henry's Commentary," Bible Gateway, March 19, 2015, https://www.biblegateway.com/passage/?search=1 Samuel 17:26-45&version=NIV. Also see *NIV – Supplementary Materials,* 402 and 395.

"WEAPONS"
1. Stephen M. Miller, "Goliath Meets a Giant-killer," *The Complete Visual Bible*, (Uhrichsville, OH: Barbour Publishing, 2011), 112.

"FAITH"
1. Matthew Henry, "1 Samuel 17," in "Matthew Henry Commentary on the Whole Bible (Complete)," Bible Study Tools, http://www.biblestudytools.com/commentaries/matthew-henry-complete/1-samuel/17.html.
2. *NIV – Supplementary Materials,* 403.
3. Matt Slick, "Why Did David Pick up Five Stones to Kill Goliath?" CARM, accessed November 14, 2014, http://carm.org/why-did-david-pick-up-five-stones-to-kill-goliath. See also Max Lucado, "Take Goliath Down!" *Facing Your Giants*, 172.
4. Miller, "Goliath Meets a Giant-killer," 112.

"DAVID"

1. Miller, "Goliath Meets a Giant-killer," 111.
2. *NIV – Supplementary Materials*, 1168.
3. Goodrick and Kohlenberger III, 1491.

"NEAR"

1. Goodrick and Kohlenberger III, *Strongest Concordance*, 1570.
2. *NIV – Supplementary Materials*, 1849.

"STEADFAST"

1. *Encyclopedia Britannica Online*, s.v. "fight-or-flight response," http://www.britannica.com/EBchecked/topic/206576/fight-or-flight-response.
2. Goodrick and Kohlenberger III, *Strongest Concordance*, 1459.
3. Goodrick and Kohlenberger III, *Strongest Concordance*, 1500. Also see "Isaiah 26:3," Bible Hub, http://biblehub.com/commentaries/isaiah/26-3.htm.
4. As referenced by Sandy Adams, "Isaiah 25–28," in "Sermon Notes," Sandy Adams, http://home.sandyadams.org/isaiah-25-28/.
5. Charles Stanley, "Healing Damaged Emotions (Part 1) – Victory Over Anxiety," (video sermon, originally aired January 20, 2013), In Touch Ministries, accessed November 14, 2014, http://www.intouch.org/watch/healing-damaged-emotions/victory-over-anxiety-video.

"YOKES"

1. *NIV – Supplementary Materials*, 1826.

"CAST"

1. Goodrick and Kohlenberger III, *Strongest* Concordance, 1570.
2. Ibid., 1602.

"GUARD"

1. Goodrick and Kohlenberger III, *Strongest Concordance*, 1582.

2. Ibid., 1562.

"DISCOVER"
1. Goodrick and Kohlenberger III, *Strongest Concordance*, 1565.
2. Ibid., 1533.
3. *NIV – Supplementary Materials*, 1816.

"BOUNDLESS"
1. See Charles John Ellicott, "Commentary on Philippians 4:13," in "Ellicott's Commentary for English Readers," 1905, http://www.studylight.org/commentaries/ebc/view.cgi?bk=49&ch=4. (Text courtesy of BibleSupport.com; used by permission.) Also see Robert Jamieson, A. R. Fausset, David Brown, "Commentary on Philippians 4:13," in "Commentary Critical and Explanatory on the Whole Bible," Studylight, http://www.studylight.org/commentaries/jfb/view.cgi?bk=49&ch=4. 1871-78. (These files are a derivative of an edition prepared from text scan by Woodside Bible Fellowship.)
2. Jonathan Merritt, "Philippians 4:13: How Many Christians Misuse the Iconic Verse," *Faith & Culture Blog*, Religion News Service, accessed October 20, 2014, http://jonathanmerritt.religionnews.com/2014/01/16/philippians-413-many-christians-misuse-iconic-verse/.

"PEACE"
1. *NIV – Supplementary Materials*, 1659.

NOTES

_____

_____

_____

_____

_____

_____

_____

_____

_____

_____

_____

_____

_____

_____

_____

_____

_____

NOTES

NOTES

_____

_____

_____

_____

_____

_____

_____

_____

_____

_____

_____

_____

_____

_____

NOTES